FROM REASON TO ROMANTICISM

From Reason to Romanticism

Reed G. Law

C. W. Post College, Long Island University

and

Bobbie W. Law

Queens College of the City University of New York

HASKELL HOUSE PUBLISHERS Ltd.
Publishers of Scarce Scholarly Books
NEW YORK, N. Y. 10012
1973

HASKELL HOUSE PUBLISHERS Ltd.

Publishers of Scarce Scholarly Books

280 LAFAYETTE STREET

NEW YORK. N. Y. 10012

Library of Congress Cataloging in Publication Data

Law, Reed G
  From reason to romanticism.

  Includes bibliographical references.
  1. Pascal, Blaise, 1623-1662. I. Law, Bobbie W.,
joint author. II. Title.
[B1903.L37 1973]   194   72-4541
ISBN 0-8383-1595-X

DEDICATED

In Loving Memory of

HARRY N. LAW

Table of Contents

.

Introduction

A TIME OF CHANGE: The period originating in the French Revolution fascinates the critic and historian of ideas because of the intensity of thought and feeling which it generated. Within the space of twenty years the profound implications of Cartesian philosophy, Newtonian science, and Rousseauistic social theory were tested in human existence. Men whose works are little known experienced the full impact of the modern condition and sketched out the ways in which man would have to deal with the paradox of his infinite capacities and his finite limitations. How did the romantic complex replace the rationalistic? The change is so total that the historian is tempted to treat it as a leap. In reality it is a perfectly normal product of the borrowing, discovering, and creating processes which go to make any age. Writers like Joseph de Maistre, Chateaubriand, and Maine de Biran were able to interiorize the ideological convulsions and adopt relevant, modern attitudes.

We shall examine the creative act of French philosophy in the years immediately following the French Revolution. The specific focus is an observation of the way in which the philosophers of this period receive the legacy of the Christian thinker, Blaise Pascal, and turn it into coin of the realm for their own times. The process by which thinkers of very different temperaments and opinions discover life and energy in the *Pensées* of Pascal and the way in which they utilize this energy to fortify their own creations form the essential content. As supernaturalists and sensualists, academicians and poets confront the fragments left by Pascal, two factors become increasingly evident: a consciousness on the part of the post-revolutionary philosophers of a need for new thoughts and new guides and second, the extraordinary plasticity of Pascal's thought. In the chemistry of these two elements may be found many of the distinctive features of the Romantic period with its elusive combinations of past and present.

To understand more precisely the issues faced by the philosopher in post-revolutionary France, we should undertake a brief review of the problems created by his immediate predecessors and the lines of investigation already in motion by the time of the Revolution. The rest of this introduction is therefore devoted to observing the atmosphere of thought prevailing then and a few errors which were becoming painfully evident.

*　*　.　*

ERRORS OF THE PAST. It is probably true that the public morality of our own times is never quite so debased as we consider it to be, nor that of our ancestors so elevated. The responsible "citizen" of revolutionary France had reason to fear the unbridled violence of his times and to cast about for moral guidance. Portalis, *orateur du gouvernement,* spoke for many of his contemporaries when he addressed the general assembly of the Corps Legislatif on the thirteenth of Germinal in the year X. Stressing the need for a return to the religious practices of former times, he inquired: "Could we regard as irreconcilable with our enlightened thought and customs a religion which great men like Descartes and Newton and many others felt honored to profess, which produced the inspired thought of a Pascal or a Bossuet and which formed the soul of Fenelon?"[1] It would appear that religious emotion cannot be instilled in a people merely by telling them that it will be good for them, or even that it had been good for someone else. The question raised by the speaker, however, marks a turning-point in the history of ideas. It announces the completion of an era of brilliant discoveries in the field of human relationships and of physical laws and points to a growing awareness that without the broader scope of religious insight man in his elusive essence slips out of control into the shadows of confusion. The inward movement of thought during the post-revolutionary period may be considered an attempt to grasp this essence in the ego itself or in the social fabric and to discover the true nature of the authority by which human actions transcend the level of mechanical gestures and animal passions.

Even without the stimulus of his observations of revolutionary violence, the post-revolutionary philosopher would have found a number of pervasive errors flowing from his predecessors. The thinker of the enlightenment was in a hurry to reach Utopia and some of his short-cuts led to precipices. Of all these errors perhaps the most deeply rooted was that of misplaced causality. The tremendous strides taken in the natural sciences by Galileo, Kepler, Bacon and Newton had implanted in the mind of the eighteenth-century *philosophe* an almost unshakable faith in the economy of the material universe whose secrets would unfold continuously before the combined forces of science and reason. That optimistic outlook might appear valid insofar as causality exists in the physical world and stands at the disposition of the human mind. It suggests a supreme cause vaguely discernible on the *outside* of reality and modeled on the organizing capacities of the intellect. But if the "natural" economy of the universe includes waste and destruction and bad faith and greed, then we must look for a general causality beyond the reach of science and human institutions or adopt attitudes of despair, which is the position eventually taken by the existentialists. Even the *philosophe* had his fleeting moments of doubt. Voltaire more than once sensed the abyss of irrationality at his feet: when the Lisbon earthquake took its toll of innocents, when the promises of Frederick the Great disappeared in a welter of dynastic wars and when his cherished Mme du Châtelet died as the result of a capricious romance. It is this failure during the Age of Enlightenment to provide an inward relationship between man and his ultimate cause that explains the subsequent reversions to intuitive patterns of thought which characterize the "Romantic Revolt."

The error induced by the expectation of finding guiding principles in the impersonal world of objects coincided with a similar error in the grounding of deism on the order of nature. Tom Paine's *Age of Reason* sums up the attempt of the deist to locate man's experience of God in the physical patterns of the universe:

> Do we want to contemplate his power? We see it in the immensity of the creation. Do we want to contemplate his wisdom? We

see it in the unchangeable order by which the incomprehensible whole is governed. . . . In fine, do we want to know what God is? Search not the book called Scripture, which any human hand might make, but the Scripture called the Creation.[2]

There is challenge and promise in the words of the rationalist, but until the human heart, mind and imagination can reach out to embrace the "incomprehensible whole," man is constrained to find other avenues of escape from the maze of his relativity. No philosopher of the French Revolution would undertake to rearrange the heroism and the horrors of those events into something befitting an orderly universe. Rational theology was not prepared to develop that sense of God in man which alone might teach him not to make himself the measure of all things. The revival of Christian theology and the popularity of social religions like those of Saint-Simon and Fourrier indicate the extent of the spiritual vacuum which had been building up to the explosion of the revolution.

The final error basic to eighteenth-century philosophers lies in the attempt to derive ethics from a romanticized view of human history. The setting is scientific. It stems originally from Newton's discovery of certain apparently fundamental laws governing the physical universe. Montesquieu's *Spirit of the Laws* and Diderot's *Natural History* suggest the carrying of Newton's technique into the study of human relationships and human nature. The assumption that detailed observation of man's behavior would lead to the formulation of a functional set of "Laws of Man" underlies the work of the Encyclopedists. If gravitation is found to be the cohesive force of material particles, what is the true force by which human societies are formed? Even the unscientific Rousseau is moved to his social writings by dreams of finding the answer to human suffering among the laws of a beneficent nature, capable of being comprehended and thus manipulated by man.

But where are the laws of human nature to be found? Condorcet logically looks for them in the history of man. As a summation of optimistic rationalism, his *Progress of the Human Mind* attributes positive and enduring values to the age of revolution. The rise and fall of past empires is interpreted as the result of a series of errors imposed on helpless masses by a few deceivers, while the future is

12

seen entrusted to the selfless concern of enlightened man who will be responsive to the rules of reason. However, if the history of man has been subject to the laws of nature in the past, there is no reason to assume that he will suddenly become their master. The inconsistency of this position was perceived by Auguste Comte:

> The work of Condorcet presents a general and continuous contradiction. On one side it proudly proclaims that civilization in the eighteenth century is infinitely superior to what it was originally. But this sum-total of progress could only be the sum of the partial advances made by civilization in all preceding ages. But, on the other side, in examining successively these different ages, Condorcet presents them almost always as having been, in the last analysis, eras of retrogression. He has on his hands, consequently, a perpetual miracle, and the advance of civilization becomes an effect without a cause.[3]

The post-revolutionary thinkers immediately set to work to clear up what appeared to be the weaknesses of their predecessors, in some cases their own early mistakes. Our investigation will review the various techniques which appear during the post-revolutionary period as an effort is made to distinguish between the quantitative masses of nature and the qualitative values of the individual and as the relationship of man to God is reformulated on a more personal basis.

* * *

THE SOURCES. As we have previously noted, the particular focal point of this study is the role of Blaise Pascal in the formation of philosophical thought in post-revolutionary France. To bring this investigation into clearer relief it is necessary to add another phase to our introduction: a summary of the attitudes running counter to the main stream of the Enlightenment. These areas contribute much to the romantic complexus and help to explain some of the immediate directions taken by thinkers during the period under consideration. In summary we shall distinguish as clearly as possible between the potential contributions of Pascal and those lines suggested by Descartes, Liebnitz, Rousseau and Kant toward the resolution of those problems faced by the early nineteenth-century philosopher.

13

The errors, or 'blind spots" of the eighteenth-century philosopher arise in large part from the failure to utilize several promising avenues for understanding opened by the previous century. Descartes, Pascal, Malebranche, Spinoza and Liebnitz disclose a new set of universals and a new psychology of man which are largely ignored until the time of Hegel and Maine de Biran. Here is a partial list of some of the syntheses which they proposed: the adaptation of Christian revelation to the psychological development of man in a scientifically defined world; the development of a sense of infinity which could give meaning to otherwise unrelated finite units or accidental combinations in a world of chaos; finally, the appeal to a purposeful divinity who alone could assure causal validity to the human will as a necessary form for the completion of the ethical act. These were the objectives of Descartes, Pascal and Leibnitz in particular, and evidence of the vitality of their thought appears in the interest which they awaken after an era which had greeted them with irony, satire and hostility.

Largely unrecognized during the eighteenth century was a basic distinction in Cartesian philosophy between the intelligence which is passive, being related to essential reality, and the will which is active, or related to experience. In spite of a troublesome inconsistency, Descartes saw his universe functioning like a machine, but his human being is a moral agent, free from the laws of necessity. The French rationalists accepted his world, but ignored his man. Perhaps most objectionable to the *philosophes* was the ontological basis of Descartes' rationalism, assuming the objective reality of ideas and placing the essence of Being in the idea of perfection:

> And further, although my knowledge grows more and more, nevertheless I do not for that reason believe that it can ever be actually infinite, since it can never reach a point so high that it will be unable to attain to any greater increase. But I understand God to be actually infinite, so that He can add nothing to His supreme perfection. And finally I perceive that the objective being of an idea cannot be produced by a being that exists potentially only, which properly speaking is nothing, but only a being which is formal or actual.[4]

The argument was introduced by Saint Anselm and continues to appear in the philosophy of Hegel and in the "living option" of William James which gives a potentially objective reality to our notion of God. The result, in Descartes' mind, was that there existed a rational approach to morality because man could conceive God, and that there was a true science of the physical universe because there was a true metaphysics. But the world perceived by the senses plays an independently valid role in the Cartesian system. It is the cause of the specific forms realized in the ideas. Thus Locke and the anti-metaphysical *philosophes* are able to erect their empirical systems entirely within this second world of Cartesian dualism. The peculiar subjectivism which characterizes Descartes' idealism and ethical thought went totally unperceived for over a century and was brought to life by pragmatists and existentialists from Biran to Sartre.

Synthesizing moral philosophy advanced a step farther in the writings of Gottfried Wilhelm von Liebnitz and then stopped short as the theorists of the Enlightenment strove inductively to derive some universal ethic from the isolated facts of human behavior. Leibnitz had suggested a law of universal continuity by adding the principle of infinitesimal calculus to the Cartesian "idea of infinity" revealing the existence of God. He observed that an indefinite number of points on a surface acquire a law of distribution when connected by a line and concluded that the indefinite series of individual substances becomes intelligible only by means of a law of continuity flowing from God, the principle of unity.[5] Morality for the individual substance therefore consists of realizing the maximum potential within its own sphere of being. For the series, perfection is a striving towards perfect balance among the parts and it was Liebnitz' fondest hope to reunite the conflicting elements of the Christian church. He sought to found this unity on the grounds of a universal ethics which would provide all the certainty of mathematics. For this reason he turned to the lofty rationalism of Saint Anselm and Descartes, using the ontological argument for the existence of God as the basis for a necessary ethics. The eighteenth-century *philosophes* were more interested in the apparent certainties of Newtonian physics, however. Not until the writings of Kant and Hegel are the questions raised by Liebnitz seriously confronted, and even then

15

with radical modifications. Kant is seeking a necessary ethics, but rejects the possibility of an ontological science. Hegel's ontology is adapted to human history and loses the individual moral significance of the Leibnitzian monadnology.

Between the systematic philosophies of Descartes and Leibnitz appears the Christian apology of Blaise Pascal. The objective of Pascal's *Pensées*, or *Thoughts*, is to kindle belief in the teachings of Christianity, rather than to extend the limits of rational comprehension. He describes in non-philosophical terms the range of human experience in an effort to persuade his hearer's heart and will to turn through desire of conviction to faith in Christianity. As the details of the *Pensées* will be analysed in the main body of this study, it is sufficient at this point to indicate some of the ways in which Pascal differs from his contemporaries.

For Pascal, human life is a phenomenon situated between the infinitely great and infinitely small. The infinite does not stand at the observable end of finite reality, however; it stands over against the finite. The finite increases or diminishes, while the infinite does not. Descartes considered finite mind related to the infinite by its capacity to conceptualize, to embrace reality. Pascal pictured a radical split between the finite and the infinite, between man and God, too great to be bridged by reason. Nor is the pre-established law of continuity an adequate explanation of human nature for Pascal. His observations of the mixed sources of human motivations preclude the singleness of purpose and total spirituality implicit in the idealism of Leibnitz. In all the systems of rationalism, man is conceived in some way to be a necessary element, standing in some relation to the source of necessity. Pascal defines man as an isolated, though contingent, unit whose only necessity is that of choosing to identify itself with finitude or with the infinite. The basic problem of human life thus becomes a moral rather than a philosophical one. The instruments by which we may enter into relationship with the infinite, according to Pascal, are the heart and Christian revelation. It is impossible for man to know God, but possible to love Him; so the experience which Pascal seeks to establish is one of faith rather than intellection.

One of the most impelling figures to color the thought of the early Romantic period is that of Jean-Jacques Rousseau. As with

Pascal, that which seems to distinguish Rousseau most clearly from his contemporaries is his preoccupation with religion and morality. We have already noted that the critical rationalists of the eighteenth century tended to turn their heavy artillery on Christianity and revealed religion, and to emphasize the utility of a rational religion in the field of ethics. In his chapter on "Civil Religion" in the *Social Contract*, Rousseau seems to acknowledge this utilitarian basis by shoring up the state on a framework of deistic theology. But in the hands of Rousseau the techniques of rationalism undergo a complete metamorphosis: the Newtonian world vanishes as the vision of the mind discovers another world in subjective feelings and conscience. An analysis of the main themes of Rousseau and Pascal will indicate their major differences and the unique appeal of each to the postrevolutionary philosopher.

Both Rousseau and Pascal base their notions of reality on the same principle of acquiring knowledge: *inner light* or *the heart which senses God*. Pascal attempts to show the complete accord between the dictates of this *inner light* and Christian theology, while Rousseau denounces all formal revelation as leading to stylized dogma and to vitiation by the distortion of human testimony. Each treats human life as paradoxical, but for each the nature of the paradox is quite different. The theme itself refers to the striking contrast between the often abject behavior of man and the tremendous potential of his vision which is capable of penetrating the mysteries of the universe and even of touching God. For Pascal the paradox is expressed in the tension between concupiscence and moral aspiration. The evil is as metaphysical as the good. Its resolution therefore lies outside of human capacities and is in fact comprehensible only in the Christian notions of original sin and salvation through Christ. Rousseau also presents life as a dichotomy of good and evil. Yet his concept of the natural goodness of man, coupled with the benevolence of Providence, leaves a mysterious evil, external to the true sources of life. The problem of evil is discussed in the *Profession of Faith of a Savoyard Vicar*, where it is attributed to the freedom accorded to man by God. It is never related to the essence either of man or of the supernatural and the question seems to be left suspended by Rousseau's isolated comment in the *Letter on Providence*: "I do not

17

see that we can seek the source of moral evil except in man, free, capable of being more perfect, yet corrupt throughout."

In their methodology Rousseau and Pascal are equally distinct. By laying heavy emphasis on the nullity of man without God and the fulfillment of man with God, Pascal creates a psychological tension requiring a resolution of the same order of reality as that of original sin and redemption. That resolution is the grace of God, and the style of Pascal is hortatory, calling the mind and emotions to a state of preparedness for the act of mercy. From *Emile* to the *Profession of Faith,* we find a world in which "All is good coming from the hands of the Author of things, all degenerates in the hands of man," a world also in which it is virtually impossible for man to establish contact with the author of goodness:

> . . . And how can we see or imagine the immensity of the great Being? When I try to rise towards Him, I do not know where I am: perceiving no relationship between Him and myself, I do not know where to find Him. I neither see nor feel anything, I find myself in empty space, and if I dared judge others by myself, I would conclude that the ecstasy of the mystics came less from an overflowing heart than an empty brain.[6]

Actually Rousseau senses the presence of God in solitary and untroubled contemplation of nature. This personal and emotional experience on the one hand tends to limit the religious experience to esthetic dimensions and on the other leads to an ethic based on the intimate voice of "conscience," that modification towards goodness brought about in senses attuned to nature. So the techniques of Rousseau lead to the cultivation of conscience through intuition: "All that I feel to be evil is evil; the best of all moral guides is the conscience."[7] He has laid bare a deep thirst for the religious experience but at the same time he has closed the avenues by which the individual might escape the vicious circle of self-contradictions. For this reason the early Romantics find in Rousseau a vague definition of life calling for the delicate application of poetic intuitions, while in Pascal lies the sharp chiaroscuro of good and evil permitting no lyrical digressions. It is not surprising that many of the post-revolutionary writers were drawn in their youth to the more kaleidoscopic effects of Rousseau.

PHILOSOPHY AND THE REVOLUTION. French philosophy on the eve of the Revolution was daring and imaginative. In reason and science it had discovered freedom; what it lacked was a principle of discipline. In Hume it had seen only a sharp critic of revealed religion and a fellow sceptic. Never do Voltaire, Diderot or Condorcet face the implications of systematic, universal scepticism. From Montesquieu to Rousseau there is an underlying assumption that proper laws would produce the good citizen and that by replacing authority with utility as the principle of government all of the evils of arbitrary control would vanish. The social philosophers whose appeals for rational government were frequently based upon an inadequate notion of reason itself should have been more receptive to Immanuel Kant. It seems unfortunate that Kant's synthesis of reason and ethics did not permeate French thought until the time of Napoleon, when it was too late.

In two important ways, however, Kant links the previous two centuries of thought with the philosophy of the Romantic period. The first deals with the favorite topic of the nineteenth century, the will, and the second with the nature of reality, the Thing-in-Itself. For Pascal, morality arose from the "reason which reason does not know." This "reason" was a mode of belief rather than intellection and resulted in a state of spiritual being. In this way volition signified an instrument for the spirit in the inner struggle against the passions, as Racine demonstrated in *Phaedra*. For the *philosophe*, the will is the instrument by which both mind and passions are able to accomplish their objectives in the social and physical world. As instrument, in the hands of analytical philosophers, the will not only loses its significance as a moral force, it disintegrates and disappears. For Condillac human behavior is the result of a biochemical process relating the senses to the world of experience: to be concerned with volition would be like considering whether a flower willed its opening in the morning. Bentham performed a similar analysis of volition as early as 1789 in the *Principles of Morals and Legislation*. Here the will, called intention, is buried between *motivation*, a group of morally neutral charges emanating from consciousness, and *consequences* which are of a public nature and to that extent moral. "But the goodness or badness of the consequences depend upon the circumstances. Now the circumstances are no objects of the intention."[8] So good and evil become external, circumstantial situations of which volition is no more than an accidental, subjective element.

Both Kant and Rousseau placed the conditions of morality not in some social end exterior to the will, but in the structure of the will itself. Rousseau finds conscience more fundamental to self-knowledge than thought: it is the spark of God in man. Kant is seeking something more explicit than this "divine instinct" of Rousseau. His "categorical imperative," or universal morality, derives with inferential necessity from the God-guarantor of a rational universe established by Descartes, but Kant, unlike the great rationalist, does not profess to have an idea of God. He identifies the will in relation to divine law: "No imperatives hold for the Divine will. . . because the volition is already of itself necessarily in unison with the law. Therefore imperatives are only formulæ to express the relation of objective laws of all volition to the subjective imperfection of the will of this or that rational being, e.g., the human will."[9] An action is good, consequently, as it conforms to the will of God, and the highest dictates of reason, not as it might achieve some immediate objective, whether useful, artistic or pleasurable. Yet if reason is the instrument for morality, it is not, as the rationalists had supposed, the instrument for knowing God. The divine being is essentially unknowable to man: for Kant the divorce is final between essence and existence and the ultimate act of reason will be an act of faith.

Among the first in France to seize upon Kant and to present him as an enemy of the Enlightenment were the mystics in the vicinity of Lyons. This movement temporarily united a number of spiritualistic or idealistic philosophers in opposition to the Encyclopedists. To a contemporary they appeared as "those mystical charlatans. . . occupied with alchemy, magic and cabal, ghosts, relations with intermediary spirits, like the Rosecrucians and the followers of Saint Germain, Cagliostro, Swedenborg and Saint-Martin." In its most positive aspirations the mysticism of the late eighteenth century constitutes an attempt to overcome, along Pascalian lines, the spiritual sterility of an exclusive and pretentious experimental science.[10] But the impelling urge of the mystic to experience total fusion of self with the deepest forces of divine activity sent many into the paths of

Buddhism, Mesmerism and Cabal. French mysticism might be considered an intense version of the religious experience which Schleiermacher defined as "the immediate consciousness of the universal existence of all finite things, in and through the Eternal."

The proclaimed chiefs of the mystics, Willermoz and Saint-Martin, certainly demand spiritual assurances of God which traditional Christianity makes no claim to grant. The search for vital sources of *pure* knowledge is pressed with urgency in all directions. From both Jacob Boehme and Martinez Pasqualis there appears a speculative, spiritual doctrine derived from ancient oriental and Christian tradition. The movement might even claim a certain philosophic universality in its search for a spiritual formula of the great-chain-of-being. Willermoz wrote in 1779 to the Christian traditionalist, Joseph de Maistre:

> If the system which is presented to you, from whatever quarter it may come, offers you a chain whose links are firmly in place and gives you a totality which explains and demonstrates to your intelligence the whole intellectual and physical universe, if it shows you your own existence as a man with all the relationships which connect you in this capacity to the rest of the universe and to its author, you must agree that it fulfills all that truth promises and that a being endowed with reason cannot refuse to adopt it if he has any taste for the truth.[11]

Here we feel the uncertainty with which the spiritually-inclined thinker at the close of the eighteenth century turned to any authority which promised to restore the validity of moral action and to reintegrate man in the kingdom of God. During the revolution the drive of mysticism is converted into Christian traditionalism by Joseph de Maistre. It reappears in the exoticism, orientalism and religious aspirations of the romantic poets. It is a force with which the philosopher of the new era must come to terms.

* * *

MEN AND IDEAS. It is easier to trace the fate of men than of ideas during the years of actual revolution. One by one the lights of reason seemed to wink out. Condorcet took poison to escape the scaffold and the poet Chénier gave up his life in rebellion against the Terror. Perhaps the confusing mixture of men and ideals may best be seen in the career of Robespierre, the "Incorruptible" disciple of the Enlightenment, the founder of a reign of Reason and Virtue and the follower of Rousseau in religious feeling, yet at the same time the father of the Terror. Historically, we might look for an explanation of the tragic waste of lives at this time in the political corruption against which Robespierre was compelled to take drastic action or in violence naturally generated by the uprooting of entrenched institutions. In any case, the terms with which he had identified himself: "reason" and "public virtue," came to be associated with the evils of the "terror" to the extent that nineteenth-century critics of the enlightenment persist in using them synonymously.

Although the popular wave of rationalism receded with the fall of Robespierre, the contradiction between the ideals of the *philosophes* and the way in which they were applied during the Revolution was not apparent to the philosophers and natural scientists under the Directoire. Daunou, Lamarck, Lavoisier, Cabanis and Tracy continue with a serene faith the non-metaphysical study of the history of man in his natural environment. Sense data remain the essential criterion of truth in the universities, although we hear that Saint-Martin was applauded at a lecture in the Ecole Normale at about this time when he asked the professor of human understanding, Garat, to stop talking about "thinking matter."[13] Apparently Garat did not take the advice and science continued to expand in chemistry, physics and the new field of psychology in the face of a renaissance of religious awareness.

The predominance of ideological over religious thought under the Directoire may probably be attributed to the fact that both the conforming and non-conforming clergy were more occupied with problems of schism and the relationship of church to state than with the formulation of faith. Unity seemed more important than doctrine as the holdings of the church were confiscated and many of the clergy who did not participate politically in the Revolution signed an oath of allegiance to the state. The active rebellion of the church against the establishment of a state religion was successful, however, and the gradual reconciliation between the Pope and the Directoire, terminat-

22

ing in the restoration of Catholicism under the Empire, far from modifying the tenets of traditional Christianity, actually clarified the issues of authority and opened a passage for religious conservatism as it sifted back into France through émigré literature early in the Romantic period.

What the Revolution accomplished, then, with respect to thought in France was to give evidence of a people freely creating its laws (the Constituent Assembly) and to complete the destruction of the political past (the convention of Danton, or of Robespierre with attempted religious reconstructions). The failure of successive parties to create a new, enduring society gave rise to bitter recriminations on the one hand and, on the other, to a frantic search for different, more efficacious principles. Both church and positive science undertook to prove their worth as social principles, and in this their aims were a far cry from those of Pascal. But in their pressing need to re-evaluate human nature and to discover new sources of religious insight they do turn to the *Pensées*, at first sceptically and then with increasing respect. It is the capacity of Pascal to triumph over tense, critical minds at this time which indicates the validity of his thought in terms of human experience and, for the first time, sets the seal of universality on his message.

The Traditionalists

Louis de Bonald (1754-1840)

One of the first and most vigorous critics of eighteenth-century political thought was Louis de Bonald, an ardent Catholic and Monarchist. Like his opponents, Bonald sought positive principles for a unified society, but his concept of social order was more nearly that of the Christian rationalists of the Middle Ages. With the Scholastics, Bonald perceived a radical distinction between cultural mores, which are man-made, and natural law, which derives from God:

> The position of the pagans was. . . false and against nature, since their customs opposed the laws of nature, and once the laws had been degraded there was no longer in society any rule by which they might be restored. Christian legislation is the only natural and reasonable way, because there the laws which come from God combat the customs of men and can, by the force of the executive sanction which accompanies them enforce and maintain public morality.[1]

As a shocked observer of the French Revolution, Bonald had both intellectual and emotional reasons for believing that any attempt to recast society about the individual must be not only false but dangerous. It is not surprising that society is considered in his works as a potential receptacle of the will of God and that the merits of given societies are judged by the extent to which they draw from God powers of stability and conservation.

Saint Thomas Aquinas saw in the permanence of the universe and of the forms which made it intelligible the unmistakable trace of a supreme intellect and universal motivating power. With the natural seeds of understanding implanted in man by God, and with the additional light of revelation, medieval aspirations towards the knowledge of God find their highest expression in his writings and a sense of the immanent disclosure of the Heavenly City runs through his works. Bonald draws his inspiration from the same source as Saint Thomas, but in terms of social forms rather than conceptual ones. From Rousseau's notion of popular sovereignty, or a free expression of the public will, Bonald turns to a sovereignty which is one and indivisible because it is derived from the nature of God. Thus Church and State become necessary mediators between man and God and the individual is defined as the particular agency by which divine law may be infused into human society.

The citizen of Bonald's society is therefore first of all a believer: "We must begin by believing something." Human reason and intuition must fail as instruments leading to belief because they proceed from individual conceptions of reality and are consequently open to debate. We should consult the whole structure of society, rather than attempt to reconstruct the parts. The primitive fact of social science for Bonald is the existence of God as generally recognized by society itself: "The general agreement or consent of mankind seems to me the strongest proof of the existence of God that can be offered to man in society."[2] The attributes of the Creator are therefore identified with the essential characteristics of the social structure: "love" which unifies mankind, "will" which sets the laws of human relationships and assures a common purpose to human strivings, and "power" which gives man the capacity to serve as an active agent of the Creator in the world. This is the comprehensive, harmonious universe of Bonald.[3] It is a universe which emerges directly from the Divine Will, like that of Hegel, but it is a "given" universe whose planets hang like Japanese lanterns in an eternal cave.

* * *

PERSONAL EXPERIENCE IN THE PHILOSOPHIES OF BONALD AND PASCAL. Bonald might well have hesitated to accept the authority of the author of the schismatic, anti-Jesuit *Provincial Letters*. His first references to Pascal in the *Journal des Curés* and the *Mélanges littéraires, politiques et philosophiques* are cautious and far from flattering.[4] As a political thinker, Bonald recoiled from the Revolution in the same way that Pascal recoiled from the Fronde. But Pascal did not turn to a dogmatic conservatism. In fact, his sister, Mme Périer tells that "He said that in a republic it is 'a great wrong to help to establish a king and oppress the liberty of the people to whom God had given it, but that in a state where royal authority was established, we could not fail to respect it without committing a sort of sacrilege, because the design of God is attached to it, not only symbolically, but as participation in the power of God' and that there is no greater evil than civil war." Certainly the author of the *Pensée:* "Royal power is founded on the good sense and on the folly of the people, particularly on the folly" (210 - Br. p. 48) is not to be considered a convinced monarchist.[5] A more consistent Thomist than Bonald, Jacques Maritain, has accused Pascal of denying or ignoring all the supreme principles of social life and of condemning man to the hopeless Jansenist doctrine: "that the sin of Adam changed man's nature and utterly corrupted everything in us." So it is interesting to observe the grounds on which Bonald comes to respect so doubtful a source.

An area in which Bonald's thinking clearly touches that of Pascal is his belief in the fundamental fact of man's fall from grace, and for both men the conviction is drawn from observation. As Pascal considers the wasted lives of the Fronde and the aimless brilliance of the *libertins,* he concludes that man without God is a confused and unhappy thing. Bonald has also witnessed misfortune in a context where religious inspiration was obviously lacking, and the portrait which he gives of his contemporaries is a biting one:

> A generation accustomed to the irreligious sarcasms of Voltaire, which yawns over the healthy humor of Molière as it falls asleep with the *Pensées* of Pascal; and it is hard to know how to instruct these sick minds, or how to amuse them.[6]

No man escapes the inward emptiness which is the heritage of original sin. Pascal observes both king and commoner attempting to lose themselves in an endless pursuit of transient pleasures. They pause only long enough to sense the unfulfilled desires which spur them on, hardly realizing that lasting satisfaction can come only from the arduous re-direction of the soul towards God from whom it has been torn, but for whom it yearns. From his own observations Bonald also defines man in terms of a fall from grace: "man is unhappy: therefore he is punished; therefore he is guilty; therefore he is no longer good." In fact there are moments when Bonald's *Théorie du pouvoir* seems to echo the Pascalian theme of the duality of human nature, compounded of flesh and spirit yet neither beast nor angel:

> Master of the universe, man is not master of himself; king of nature, his sovereignty has the fragility of a reed and tearing prick of a thorn; the imposing exterior of human dignity hides only shameful weaknesses or the infirmities of nature. . . . YES. . . That is man.[7]

* * *

SOCIAL PESSIMISM AND OPTIMISM. If physical and moral weakness characterize the individual social unit, what hopes may we entertain for the social structure in general? Here the political pessimism of Pascal is thoroughly consistent, as he resolves the question of social forms on the more fundamental plane of Christian doctrine. Man may seek for justice in his political institutions, and it is well: "Thirst for justice: eighth beatitude," since a thorough search must lead to God. Social justice has always fallen so far short of our desires that, "unable to bring it about that what is just should be strong, we have made strength just" (416 - Br. p 298). The desire for fulfillment which has prompted man to create social organizations does not prove the validity of any one of them. On the contrary, the fact that no human institution has been able to provide a clear and true pattern of justice seems to indicate that man should go beyond and consult the message of revealed religion. Bonald follows Pascal's description of humanity, but in keeping with the spirit of his age he remains a social optimist and moralist. So in the *Théorie du pouvoir* the physical-spiritual duality of human nature is found to require a dual system of checks:

> The passion for domination, natural in man, irritated and aroused in society by the presence of objects and the frequency of opportunities, can be controlled only by the double force of political power. . . [and religion]. Religion checks the individual wills and the government checks the outward actions.[8]

27

In this way Louis de Bonald lays the theoretical groundwork for the revival of monarchy in France. While Napoleon was accustoming the French mind to renounce freedom in favor of equality under authority, Bonald sought to reconcile the notion of authority with that of constitutional monarchy. He is pleased to find Montesquieu's definition of this system as a government "where a single person governs, but by fixed and established laws." But by whom are the laws fixed? If man-made, what assurance of universal justice can they give? If prescribed by God, where are they revealed? In answer to these questions Rousseau referred to man in his presocial condition and suggested that the ideal lawmaker would be a philosopher who had discarded the artificial class systems of Europe and who could reproduce the original spirit of man in the state of nature. Bonald is more characteristic of nineteenth-century attitudes by defining man in terms of the natural evolution of organized society:

> So nature should be the only legislative power of societies: and it is actually the only legislator of organized societies, whose authorities have only to draw up, in written law, the customs which the general will of society or nature have established, or to make the changes which nature shows to be necessary.[9]

The ideal "secretaries of nature" have been bestowed on France in the persons of Clovis, Charlemagne and Saint Louis. France may have been ready to welcome a Charlemagne by the 1820's, but it received instead Charles X. By identifying eternal religious truths with a specific form of government, Bonald placed both church and state in a vulnerable position from which neither could extricate itself during the century to follow. The tragic consequences will be seen in the fate of the last traditionalist, Félicité de Lammenais.

* * *

HUMAN NATURE DEFINED. The path which leads Bonald most directly back to Pascal lies in his definition of man and the agencies through which human nature is brought to complete realization. In both the *Mélanges* and *Recherches philosophiques* he is concerned with refuting the sensualist interpretation of man's knowledge and ethical motivation. One of his favorite phrases: "man is an intellect served by organs," is obviously a refutation of Condillac and the school of empiricism which would describe all the operations of the mind in terms of sense data. To Bonald, man's capacity for intellection distinguishes him from the physical universe, and this distinction he found to be underlined by Pascal:

> It is therefore solely by intelligence that man is the master of the physical universe, and that he is superior to all material objects, 'all our dignity,' said Pascal, 'lies in thought.'[10]

Then how shall we identify human nature? Is it the disembodied intellect, fallen into some alien environment? Life appears rather to be a flux between the mind which guides physical activity and the sense organs which stir the mind to action. Bonald moves in the direction of extreme rationalism as he concludes in De l'organisation corporelle that the "principle which wills in us is totally distinct from the faculty which produces movement." What he must discover is an ethical principle in which both mind and body would be related in some functional design. Otherwise the human condition becomes by definition totally incomprehensible: a unity of unrelated parts.

To resolve his dilemma Bonald turns to the Pensées. Pascal had isolated three categories of being; body, mind and will. Through the body we participate in the relativity and change of the world, through the mind we are aware of our impermanence and attempt to establish contact with the permanent, and through will we induce in the mind and body those acts of faith and love which permit us to achieve identity as a conscious creature of God. Without the religious explanation human nature is self-contradictory.and Pascal concludes Section VI of the Pensées:

> Let man now know his proper price. Let him love himself, for he has a nature capable of good, but let him not therefore love the vileness it contains. . . . He has in him the capacity to know the truth and to be happy; but he possesses no truth, either permanent or satisfactory. . . . I would then lead man to long to find some truth, to be ready, free from passions, to pursue till he finds it, knowing how greatly his knowledge is darkened by passions. . . . All these contradictions, which threatened to carry me further from knowledge of religion, are what have led me soonest to true religion (207-209, Br. pp. 516-517).

So for Pascal the dialectical method is justified by the structure of human nature: a unity emerging from opposing forces. The truth of man is found in a psychic, if not metaphysical, tension. Bonald uses the same psychological approach to the problem of identification in the *Mélanges*, where he elaborates on the *Pensées*: "Man is truly no more than extremes and contradictions. Such as he is in his original state, he is made up of extreme qualities, opposed by the contrary combinations of strength and weakness, of heights and depths. . . ." In spite of his firm stand against philosophic rationalism, Bonald is unwilling to relinquish a persistent faith in the capacity of reason to bring the universe into a true harmony and to control the irrational. Of Pascal's three orders of being, therefore, Bonald chooses two: will and mind. Will represents the order of divine law which assures the stability of the created universe; Mind represents the order of human reason where the divine law is transfused into the institutions of organized society. Only after his consideration of Pascal's description of the interplay of rational and irrational forces does Bonald seem to sense the enigmatic quality of experience and the religious significance of the enigma: "As he might be by the progress of his reason, man is composed of extreme qualities in harmony through their opposition. . . That is the mystery of man, the secret of the arts, the very teaching of religion."[11]

Pascal's three orders, or categories of being, imply corresponding faculties: physical, rational and religious. The faculty through which the religious experience is accomplished is the "heart." If he ignores this faculty, man stands on the brink of an abyss, between the aspirations of his reason and the conflicting demands of his body and senses. Without a sense of religion, the most accomplished scientist may contemplate the laws of the universe and still ask: "Why am I here, and why do I wonder why I am here?" So the most perfectly balanced personality is to be found in men of humble minds who have been touched by God's grace:

And therefore those upon whom God has bestowed religion by cordial feeling [sentiment du coeur] are very fortunate, and are quite fairly convinced. But to those who lack religion we can only give it by process of reason, waiting till God makes it felt by the heart, without which faith is but human, and unavailing for salvation (630 Br. 460).

This completes the cycle of Pascal's thought. The present condition of human nature; the ability of the intellect to embrace the physical universe, yet incapable of knowing what God is; the weakness of the body, doomed to the life and death patterns of nature itself; all testify to the fall of man from grace. The endless succession of philosophical and political systems further demonstrates the continuing desire of man to discover the real source of truth and justice. Finally, the religious experience of the humble and devout heart shows the re-integration and fulfillment possible through the gift of faith.

In his epistemology Descartes conceived the notion of an infinite will which perpetually nourished and guaranteed the finite will of man. Bonald proposed to apply the same principle to the theory of the formation of society. The bulk of his work is therefore devoted to a process of analogy in which he posits the essential characteristics of a God-legislator and derives from them the corresponding essentials of the state: because God is power, for example, so must government be vested with power as an agency of divine purpose. If man is free, however, his institutions need not reflect the direct action of God. At times his arbitrary structure totters and Bonald recognizes that man is made for tragedy as well as for salvation through his social institutions. The vicissitudes of personal experience must be taken into account. The first serious doubts concerning the uniformity of man's responsiveness to the "fixed and established laws" of his God-legislator appear in the *Théorie du pouvoir*:

> The reader will find in some portions of this work a perhaps fatiguing number of oppositions and antitheses: it is a particular inconvenience of the subject with which I am dealing. The antithesis is in the words only because there is opposition in the things. Placed between the *general will* of society and the particular *will* of man, that is to say between the constitution of man perfected by society and the institutions of degenerate man or of his passions, I find myself constantly between two extremes, I am always walking between being and nothingness.[12]

What is it in man from which society is formed? Where logic fails to provide consistent forms for drawing up a comprehensive social theory, one may turn to religion and it is here that Bonald finds the order, universality and illumination for which he was looking.

Viewed from the debris of the Revolution, the failure of the rational systems of the eighteenth century to unlock the secrets of human motivation and to expose the true laws of man's relationship to man seemed prophetic to Bonald. So the religion to which he turns is not of the Christian rationalists where the laws are apprehended through intellect: "Religion, which is *intelligence* for some, is *love* for all; because all men do not have enlightened minds, but all have responsive hearts."[13] Here Bonald's experience of the Revolution leads him to the central theme of Pascal: that without the ingredient of love, the most carefully designed social system will remain empty and lifeless.

Bonald, like the other traditionalists whose works follow, was primarily concerned with the preservation of Christian doctrine and of the Catholic Church which he considered threatened by materialism and democratic social theory. The apologetic intention of his work sometimes produces weaknesses in the development of his philosophical vision. At first he defends Pascal simply because it was Pascal, more than any other spokesmen for Christianity, whom Voltaire undertook to refute. He was not prepared to take up the "Jansenist problem" at a time when the Church appeared to require unity. Still he has set out to "instruct the sick minds" of his generation, and he makes more and more frequent use of Pascal's striking analysis of the aspirations and contradictions at work in man. This is the first step. Gradually Pascal attains the status of an authority in the *Théorie du pouvoir* and the Pascalian paradox of the greatness and misery of man plays a considerable role in the *Recherches philosophiques*, until Bonald's own faith in static, divinely-inspired laws of society touches Pascal's sense of God perceptible to the human heart. Bonald is primarily a man of his age and his mind is beset with contemporary problems, but he has clearly drawn Pascal into the orbit of thought where basic attitudes are formed and resolutions determined.

JOSEPH DE MAISTRE (1753-1821)

During the early, hectic years of Restoration under Louis XVIII, the rising forces of religious traditionalism and political conservatism found a powerful ally in Joseph de Maistre. As Chateaubriand and Lamartine produced an atmosphere favorable to a revival of Christian feeling, Bonald, Maistre and Lamennais undertook to restore the institutions and doctrines of the Catholic Church and monarchy. It is not by chance that Maistre submitted an early copy of his book *Du Pape* to Lamennais through the offices of Lamartine. The brilliant success of the *Conservateur* from 1818 to 1820 combined the talents of Bonald, Lamennais, Fiévée, Chateaubriand, Fayet and Lamartine. This group more than any other seemed to be a guiding spirit under which France would regain its cultural unity and vigor. It called for a monarchy of unlimited powers and a church submissive to the authority of Rome. The movement appealed to Maistre's search for logic and harmony in society and religion and to it he offered his vision of the underlying forces from which French history and tradition derived its unity. The death of Maistre in 1821 preceded the triumph of Hugo in popular religious thought and the storm which left Lamennais excommunicated. His *Soirées de Saint Pétersbourg* may therefore be considered the purest, and probably the most profound, document of the traditionalist movement.[1]

Following Bonald, Maistre pictures the Revolution as a night of torment and disordered dreams following a long day of reasonable stability under the established order of unquestioned authority. But for Bonald the tragic flaw was a structural one which could be repaired by a return to the eternal patterns by which France had evolved to her cultural maturity. For Maistre the problem of revolution and restoration is an essentially moral one, to be resolved through expiation, conversion and redemption. In that sense, "One of the greatest crimes that one can commit is that which is directed against sovereignty, none having more disastrous consequences." So the French nation as a whole had taken upon itself the guilt of putting to death an innocent man, Louis XVI, and at the same moment incurred the inevitable suffering of a society with no legitimate leadership. Expiation had been swift and terrible under the Terror

33

and would presumably continue unless the nation recognized her guilt and submitted to an act of faith through which the kingdoms of man and God were restored to their rightful places. These are the themes of Maistre's earlier works, *Considérations sur la France, Sur la souveraineté, Du Pape* and *L'Eglise gallicane:* the recognition of a communal guilt, the identification of this present guilt with the whole history of man's criminal rebellion against the prescribed order of Providence, and the investigation of ethical attitudes by which man might be reconciled to the demands of Providence. Since truth lies entirely within the province of God and error in the history of man, the position of Joseph de Maistre is forcefully summed up by Faguet: "The revolutionary dialecticians drew up the rights of man and Maistre the declaration of the rights of God."

* * *

MAISTRE'S POLITICAL THEORY AND THE ROLE OF PASCAL. The key to Maistre's political and religious outlook is to be found in his interpretation of the role of Providence in human affairs. The controlling force within whose established boundaries the history of man fluctuates constitutes an ethical absolute, a categorical imperative, impenetrable to human reason. In the *Considérations sur la France,* Providence appears as the implacable incarnation of moral law operating through the nature of things and radically opposed to the prejudiced courts of human justice. Its verdicts need not be executed within the confines of time, since its nature is eternal, but in the case of a crime of national dimensions as with the Revolution, it may be swift to punish.[2] If we are to understand the nature of society in the light of this conception of Providence, we shall arrive at the following conclusions: That constitutions evolve naturally from the given characteristics of a social group and are not susceptible to revision by individual human reason, and that Providence tends to maintain that which it created and to punish that which attempts to disrupt its creation (Chapt. VI). The longevity of a political institution may be therefore interpreted as the sign, if not the seal, of divine approbation, while schism and political violence is clearly the product of human interference with the natural

34

order of society. The Roman Empire and French monarchy did not fall of their own corruption; they were destroyed by small groups of self-willed men who devoted their talents to the creation of some new social order more congenial to their private aspirations, instead of encouraging necessary modifications in the old "True Order." Reaching beyond the goals of Bonald, Maistre's concept of Providence transcends conservative apologetics and enriches the history of religious thought as it gradually encounters the "hidden God" of Pascal.

As a monarchist Maistre was faced with the problem that French monarchic society did not possess a Magna Charta nor any specific documents establishing the legitimate relationship between the governing and the governed. It was by raising the question of the contractual validity of the Ancien Régime that Montesquieu and Rousseau created the atmosphere of revolution. By contrast the political theorist of the eighteenth century called for a clearly defined social compact designed to fulfil the aspirations of each contractant. To this extent Hegel follows the line of thought set down by Rousseau when he considers the Law or State to be an expression of the social, rational projects of man. The originality of Hegel lies in the fact that for him the projects are not the fragmentary structures produced by man's egotistical impulses, but intrinsic, necessary qualities of social life. It appears that Joseph de Maistre's position touches that of Hegel on many points: the notion of a universal sovereignty through whose action society is born, and the profession of governmental absolutism. Yet in the ultimate movement of their thought we find Hegel moving in the direction of a pure superstate and Maistre in that of a pure Christian theocracy.

With Hegel, Joseph de Maistre totally repects Rousseau's conception of the contractual origin of the State. For both, the choice implied in a compact between the individual and society is as ridiculous as a choice between being and non-being: if man is a social animal it is not due to the fact that he chose to be social any more than that he chose to be animal. Therefore liberty is not, as the eighteenth century had supposed, a question of choice, but of the adaptation of the individual to the necessary form of society. The State for Hegel is not merely a guardian of individual liberty, but a *primary, objective liberty* in itself, from which individual lives derive significance. Maistre, however, remains closer to the position which we have identified in Pascal, where the State is considered an appendage of the Divine Will, with authority only in relation to the physical life of man, while religion contains the most direct expression of Divine Will and constitutes authority in the life of the spirit. Contrary to Hegel, then, Mastre holds the State to be a *relative*, or *secondary, objective liberty*. This distinction is fundamental to Maistre's political thought and may be directly attributed to the way in which he, like Pascal, examines the fact of society *a posteriori*, in reference to the underlying truth of Christianity.

The absolutism of Hegel presupposes the truth of a theme which was popularized by Mme de Staël in the early nineteenth century: the perfectibility of man in his proper setting. For Maistre the conditions under which the drama of human history is enacted are modified by original sin:

> There is nothing but violence in the universe; but we have been spoiled by modern philosophy which has said that *all is well*, while evil has corrupted everything, and while in a very real sense, *all is evil*, since nothing is in its proper place. As the tonic note of creation has been lowered, all the others have descended according to the rules of harmony. *All creatures tremble* and turn, with pain and suffering, towards another order of things.[3]

In a universe where evil is rooted in the essence of things, no human instrument or organization can be expected to rise above the levels established by Providence. From a similar hypothesis Pascal concluded that while man has succeeded in drawing up excellent laws for controlling his selfish interests, "in reality that ugly root of man, the 'evil substance' is only covered up; it is not taken away." Maistre would go even a step beyond Pascal in *Sur la souveraineté*, to declare the complete helplessness of human reason in the formation of institutions:

> Human reason reduced to its individual capacities is perfectly useless, *not only for the creation, but even for the conservation of all religious or political associations*, because it produces only disputes, and because man, in order to conduct himself properly, does not need problems, but beliefs.[4]

If the critics of Maistre's political theory find a paradoxical juxtaposition of an apology for established authority and the denial of any rational justification for this authority, we may assume that for Maistre, as for Pascal, truth is necessarily paradoxical in a system whose order has been perverted through the fall from grace.

With such a metaphysical understanding of the relationship of political systems to the works of Providence, Maistre can agree with Pascal "that he would have as much horror of destroying civil liberty where God has bestowed it as he would of introducing it where it had not been before" (Quotation in *Du Pape, Oeuvres II*, p. 9). For him, as for Pascal, an objective judgment of different concrete political organizations is almost impossible, since all draw their substance from God and participate in the life and death cycles of history. Only the more liberal of his aristocratic contemporaries could approve the American constitution or applaud the English nation as sincerely as Maistre: "Only a people born to enjoy liberty could have demanded the Magna Charta; and the Magna Charta would have been useless for a people to whom freedom was indifferent." Maistre's defense of monarchy in France therefore stands upon the sole ground that it is the most faithful representation of the natural characteristics of the French people. The Revolution does not demonstrate the inadequacy of monarchy as much as the existence of a superior and more inexorable law: that the nature of political institutions is not rational and will not withstand the test of rational analysis: "If the moral mechanism of empires were made manifest, we would be disabused of a number of errors." This sense of pessimism, or realism, which pervades Maistre's thought is ultimately hostile to his apology for the monarchic system. In detail, about the best that he can find to say of it is that it usually recognized true talent and worth, and that in any case it was preferable to the chaos of the abortive republic *(Sur la souveraineté, Oeuvres I*, pp. 481-482).

As Cagordan has pointed out, the originality of Joseph de Maistre does not lie in his defense of the *ancien régime*, but in his demonstration of man's incapacity to improvise anything of enduring value in the organization of society.[5] We have already seen that this scepticism comes from a Pascalian sense of original sin whose action has so perverted the order of things that human reason alone is unable to resolve the enigma. We have also noted the appearance in Maistre's works of the Pascalian paradox, according to which man is perpetually searching for the unity which would complete his contingent existence, but which is not to be found on the inferior level of human institutions. It is not surprising therefore to find Maistre concluding that man's fundamental unity is religious in a way which is highly reminiscent of the *pensée* on the misery and greatness of man:

> Man in conjunction with his Creator is sublime, and his action is creative; on the contrary, as soon as he separates himself from God and acts alone, he does not cease to be powerful, for that is a privilege of his nature; but his action is negative and tends to destroy.[6]

We shall examine Maistre's religious thought in its definitive form in the *Soirées de Saint-Pétersbourg* where the spirit of the *Pensées* is subtly adapted to the most urgent philosophic problems of the early nineteenth century.

* * *

MAISTRE'S CRITICISM OF PASCAL AND SCIENCE. Before passing with too much confidence to this examination, we should recognize that most of Maistre's direct references to Pascal are aggressively hostile. In the revival of the dispute between Jesuits and Jansenists at the turn of the century, considerable importance was attached to the *Lettres Provinciales*, and Maistre felt impelled to deal severely with them. In both his *Du Pape* and *Eglise gallicane* he attacks Pascal for his Jansenism, and in the second *entretien* of the *Soirées de Saint-Pétersbourg* he refers disparagingly to the *Menteuses de Pascal*. Dwelling upon the inconsistencies and contradictions to be found in the works of Pascal, Maistre treats him with the same irreverence accorded elsewhere to John Locke. In his chapter, "Pascal considered from the triple point of view of science, literary merit and religion" *(Eglise gallicane)*, Maistre makes light of Pascal's accomplishments in experimental physics and sketches a dialogue between Pascal and his *directeur de conscience* in which the latter succeeds in defending the integrity of the Jesuit order. In the *Du Pape*, he opposes the defender of the schismatic sect to the author of the *pensée*, "We must not judge what the Pope is by a few words of the Fathers. . . , but by the acts of the Church and of the fathers, and by the canons." Much of this antagonism occurs in a context where Maistre is supporting one of the most controversial issues of the Church in the first half of the nineteenth century: the infallibility of the Pope. On this vital, although isolated, issue Pascal is in the camp of the enemy. We shall see that the difference of opinion on this specific issue does not prevent Maistre from fully appreciating the religious insights of the *Pensées*.

In the dialogue form of the *Soirées de Saint-Pétersbourg*, Joseph de Maistre makes one of the most comprehensive attempts in the annals of thought during the Romantic period to consolidate the undeniable contributions of the eighteenth century to human progress under the guiding principles of a reinvigorated Christianity. From Newton to Lavoisier, man's understanding of the physical universe had expanded furiously, but at the same time his spiritual curiosity had declined at a corresponding rate. Likewise, the application of scientific techniques to the interpretation of the Bible served only to obscure the ethical core of traditional Christianity, rather than bringing new light to bear upon it. And finally a large portion of the intuitive wisdom embodied in the articles of Christian faith was identified with superstition and rejected in favor of rational deism or humanism. For this reason Maistre undertakes to reassign science and biblical criticism to their proper place in the orders of understanding and to restore the validity of Christian ethics and faith as legitimate factors in human experience.

The nature of scientific truth, and in what area of human understanding its conclusion can be said to constitute laws draws Maistre, as we have noted, into the philosophical field of debate. To demonstrate the ethical validity of revealed truth, as opposed to the inhuman logic of physical or mathematical systems, the author of the *Soirées* evokes the warmth of conviction to be found in a Pascalian interpretation of the heart:

But these truths (of revelation) cannot be proved by mathematics nor by the laws of movement. He who has spent his life without ever having tasted the things of God, he who has limited his mind and dried up his heart by sterile speculations which can neither make him better in this life nor prepare him for another life, this person, I say, will reject this sort of proof and will see nothing in them. There are some truths that man can grasp only with *the understanding of his heart*.[7]

This theme alone permits Maistre to avoid a pitfall into which many of his contemporaries fell: the reliance upon "common consent" to prove the truth of first principles. For Kant and Bonald, for traditionalists and eclectics, the existence of God was sufficiently demonstrated by the universal acceptance of this notion by human societies everywhere. The atheist would therefore merely have to prove his humanity in order to discredit the principle. Maistre has chosen a broader basis for his ethical system by freeing the individual from a strict intellectual relationship to first principles. This would account for the possibility of persons with equal mental capacities either to accept or reject the notion of God. So the atheist does not demolish the rational structure of truth when he denies the existence of God: he simply exerts his ethical privilege of refusing to make this choice of the "heart," "proving nothing more than his individual misfortune." What may be rejected by some through intellectual reservations and by others through sensuality must nevertheless be available to all if morality is to have any universal significance. In a footnote where he defends Pascal against Voltaire, Maistre indicates his comprehension of the nature of the heart and the unique claims of Christianity in the development of this faculty:

> What does it matter that a man has uttered a few obscure words about *the love of God?* It is not a matter of *talking* about it, it is a question of *having* it; it is even a question of inspiring it in virtue of a general institution, available to all sorts of minds. Now that is what Christianity has done, and what philosophy has never done nor can do. We cannot repeat it enough: it cannot win over the hearts of men.—*Circum praecordia ludit.* It plays about the heart; it never enters.[8]

* * *

THE TRUE RELIGION. If Pascal and Maistre have found a common cause concerning the ethical nature of man, the privileged position of Christianity is much less obvious to the nineteenth century than it was to the seventeenth. Two obstacles stand between the

40

Pensées and the *Soirées:* the biblical criticism of the eigtheenth century and the new appreciation of oriental religions. We have seen that Maistre rejects rational analysis of revealed truths on the grounds that it ignores the intuitive basis upon which such truths are acquired. But in the midst of prevalent oriental and apocalyptic influences, and well-informed as to the homogeneity of all religious symbolism through his initiation in illuminism, he is inclined to take the more liberal position that all religions draw their portion of truth from a common source. In his apology for Christianity Maistre treads a delicate path between the confining walls of dogmatism and the soaring peaks of mysticism, both of which hold an obvious fascination for him. Much of the balance which he is able to achieve is due to his close consultation of Pascal in the selection of criteria for a "true religion."

Pascal was intensely aware that the ultimate objective of religion is the creation of a bond between man and God. The major obstacle to this union, however, lies in man's need to judge the eternal pattern of life in terms of his own finite conception of reality and his natural inclination to bestow his love upon objects which are extensions of his own personality, his possessions, or which reflect his personality in a desirable way. Few men are capable of a sustained relationship with a being whom they cannot know and whose merits are self-contained. A true religion should therefore explain the detachment of mankind from God and suggest a remedy by which the gulf could be bridged. The Judaic-Christian tradition distinguishes itself from other religions and philosophical systems by defiring the isolalation of mankind on the ethical grounds of human guilt: "We are born so hostile to (the) love of God, and it is so essential, that we must be born guilty; else God would be unjust" (360 - Br. p. 554). Only by recognizing the fact of guilt can man refrain from considering himself as an *ens causa sui* and suspend his judgments of God. All religions may attempt to guide man towards an ideal, but only Christianity expresses the nature of ethical struggle implicit in a complete doctrine of the heart. It is this faculty which reveals the inadequacy or unworthiness of the self as a moral objective and which at the same time offers an instrument by which man may acquire intuitive love and understanding of the will of God.

41

The sight of human suffering brought many eighteenth-century deists to the brink of militant atheism. Voltaire's *Candide* and *Poème sur le désastre de Lisbonne* frequently rose to haunt the religious thinkers of the Romantic period. There are in fact several curious documents presented by Pierre Leroux and Jean Reynaud in the first half of the nineteenth century in which Pascal is generally supported against Voltaire, but in which Voltaire's view of human suffering would appear to be vindicated when Reynaud, in the third chapter of *Terre et Ciel*, suggests that the earth is actually Hell and that the pains of life on earth are compensated by various forms of bliss on other planets.[9] But even if they are to be rewarded in some after-life, how can the obvious misery of innocent victims be correlated with divine justice? With Pascal, Maistre finds new reasons in observing that in the course of human affairs "there are no lives which may be considered pure and justified in their own right." The phases of existence which are repulsive in the light of reason may be understood and assimilated by a humble heart. Maistre finds in Christianity the same unique reconciliation of suffering with the love of God as that pointed out by Pascal: "The contrite heart is not to be found in other religious systems, they have never learned to ask forgiveness in their prayers."[10]

Apart from the passages in which Pascal comes to grips with the most anguishing obstacles to faith, the *Pensées* indicate three secondary marks of a true religion: "perpetuity, the good life and miracles." This is the aspect of religion which may not provoke conviction, but which supports and strengthens the primary movement of the heart. Maistre must therefore have arrived at a degree of persuasion close to that of Pascal before approaching the demonstrative portion of his apology. The details of this demonstration clearly echo the criteria of the *Pensées*. Christianity may be seen in its intimate relationship with the Hebrew tradition, growing out of the earliest records of a sense of God in man and retaining a doctrine essentially independent of the cultures through which it has passed. From this, Maistre concludes that "if Christianity were human, its teachings would vary with human opinions; but as it derives from the unchanging, it is unchanging also." A valid religion should incline the believer toward a more perfect order of things and modify

42

his personality for living "the good life." So, summing up his observations of the range of human attitudes, from the noble to the most sordid, Maistre invites his reader to see "how each dogma of Christianity is attached to the fundamental laws of the spiritual world; it is equally important to note that there are none which do not tend to purify man and exalt him."[11]

Pascal's proximity to the miraculous healing of his niece during the troubled days of Port-Royal perhaps led him to place more emphasis on the role of miracles in the acquisition of faith than we might expect from an apologist who has made every effort to evoke the religious content of general human experience. Yet in spite of his special insight, he is careful not to make miracle the criterion of religious truth so much as the seal of a profound doctrine: "Miracles are for the sake of doctrine and not doctrine for the sake of miracles" (Adversaria 98 - Br. p. 720). Maistre hesitates to separate isolated miracles from the miraculous forms of life itself, and never discusses them beyond the rather curt comment that "God offers no useless ones." On the other hand, Maistre finds a broader basis for belief in the accomplishment of the prophecies than did Pascal. The latter avoids a theological debate over the literal fulfilment of the prophecies of the Old Testament in the person of Christ, and considers them primarily as prefigurations of the collapse of the old empires and kingdoms and the establishment of a new religion in Jerusalem and Rome.[12] According to Maistre, "Man is subjected to time; although by nature he is a stranger to time." Man's knowledge is of the past and his projects are of the future; he is prophetic by nature. Even the obscure passages of the prophets constitute testimony for this extra-temporal portion of common human experience, and furnish a valid basis for the claims of Christianity.

* * *

PESSIMISM AND THE WILL TO BELIEVE. Many modern critics and philosophers have objected to any attempt to establish Christian truths on grounds of philosophical pessimism and scepticism. If no ethical or ideological system is coherently justifiable in itself, then a thinker who accedes to any source of authority would seem to have abdicated his intellectual integrity.

In his book on *Pascal et notre coeur,* Daniel-Rops confesses: "We must admit that a grieving and disturbed Pascal casts a more moving spell than the dogmatic Pascal, taken up with demonstrations and wagers. The consequences of the confidence which I placed in him occurred to me only after much debate and hesitations, much later."[13] Faguet accuses with his customary irony the contrast between a sense of injustice, of evil in the world, and the thirst for simplicity which motivated Maistre's search for truth and his apparently prosaic, undemanding conclusion which "rests and is content in Christianity."[14] Yet in the form which pessimism takes with Pascal and Maistre and in the role to which they assign the will in the acquisition of faith, it is clear that doctrine always remains subordinate to intellectual and moral attitudes which can never acquire the passive perfection of doctrine. In the *Pensées* and the *Soirées,* Christianity represents less an ultimate submergence of thought than a method of identifying the unending processes of self-understanding and self-domination.

From Sénancour and Kierkegaard to Nietzche, the nineteenth century was productive of pessimists whose accents touched every chord from irony to desperation. Most of the major themes characterizing this pessimism already appear in the poetry of Alfred de Vigny: the injustice or indifference of God manifested in human suffering, in the *Fille de Jephté;* the vulgarity of man and the indifference of nature, in the *Maison du Berger;* the inevitable isolation of a superior intellect among men, in *Moïse;* and the corrupt condition of human nature, in the *Colère de Samson.*[15] In this sense, pessimism is the discovery of an imbalance between things as they are and as they should be, and the ultimate objective of the pessimist is to indicate the grounds upon which some sort of restitution should be made. Both Vigny and Nietzsche were deeply impressed by Pascal's bitter vision of physical reality and his sense of a Providence withdrawn behind "the eternal silence of infinite space." But Vigny seeks within himself the dignity and causality which the "ready-made" terms of life would deny, while Nietzsche translates this same affirmation of self into his concept of the superman. In both cases, however, an effort of will is necessary to overcome the repressive ac-

44

tion of nature and society and to establish the rights of self. At the very beginning of this movement, Maistre suggests a typically Pascalian rejection of self as a worthy objective of the dedicated struggle of the will, the refusal to accept any triumph on a lesser level than that of hidden Providence itself.

The Jansenist doctrine of "efficacious grace" and the cautious bestowal of it on a chosen few was thoroughly unpopular with the nineteenth-century moralists who would like to embrace as wide a range of humanity as had the eighteenth-century rationalists. Maistre is neither the first nor the last to accuse Nicole and the Port-Royalists of ignoring the importance of the will and of leading "from discouragement to rebellion or despair, while waiting for grace and desire." It was certainly a temptation for him to accept the planned approach to religious conviction outlined in Saint-Martin's *man of desire*: "Man is a desire of God, who would instill in him a marvellous ethical force, and man should be a man of desire, by his cultivation within himself of these divine elements."[16] But Maistre has already discovered that man "cannot desire what he does not know," and that desire can never be more than an inclination of the will which in itself contains no mystical powers capable of setting in motion the benevolent forces of Providence.

In fact, both Maistre and Pascal recognize in the human will a blind power through which the contingent ego is attached to some object which promises it the fulfilment it is incapable of supplying in itself. According to Pascal, it is not a selective instrument, but rather one of self-preservation:

> The Will is one of the principle agents of belief; not that it creates belief, but because things are true or false according to the side from which we look at them. The Will, preferring one aspect to another, turns the Mind away from contemplating the qualities of things which possess qualities it does not care to see; and so the Mind, walking in step with the Will, stops to look at the aspect it likes; it comes to a stand before the aspect it prefers, and so it forms judgment by what it sees therein (369 - Br. p. 375).

Maistre uses the deists as an example of those whose wills have chosen human understanding as the final object of belief. Their misfortune is therefore that, like Dante's "undecided" in Limbo, they

45

cannot will their own regeneration, because "they find in their own moral mists some peculiar fascination which is a frightful punishment."[17] It is only with the phenomenon of moral suffering that man is forced to project his finite longings beyond the boundaries of finite recompense. By his suffering alone man indicates that he has not given up the struggle, but that he is determined to regain the highest forms of life. This is no esoteric doctrine, based upon mystical experience; it is a statement of will made humble by uncertainty, unwilling to glorify an unglorious object: "Man must act as though he could do nothing. That is the fatal conclusion of wisdom." Maistre has learned through Pascal that the triumph of volition lies in the sustained effort to deny the stimuli of self and pursue the valid substance of the will of God.

Pascal indicates two ways in which this process of volition may be experienced: outwardly, as the denial of self in commitments to society through acts of charity, and inwardly, as the denial of self in commitments to God through prayer. An aristocrat of the intellect, Maistre is more concerned with the second of these themes and the sixth *entretien* of his *Soirées* indicates complete accord with Pascal that "God would rather bend the will than the mind. Perfect insight would help the mind but harm the will. Down with pride." And since understanding is essentially the result of a moral discipline of the mind, Maistre concludes his reflections on the validity of the will by quoting the *pensée* that God has established prayer "to communicate to his creatures the dignity of causality." Pascal saw the life of man, then, as a physiological and intellectual structure, condemned to destruction unless it could sink its roots into the life-giving soil of Christian doctrine. Maistre renews the attempt to revitalize nineteenth-century philosophy by reproducing the Pascalian concept of ethical effort at the base of human understanding. In our chapter on Maine de Biran we shall see a similar movement take place with respect to the physiology of the will.

It is clear that the traditionalist was as concerned with the restoration of Christian theology and Christian society as with a rebirth of Christian religion. Maistre was schooled by the Jesuit order and converted from gallicanism to ultramontanism. There was certainly no emotional reason for him to look for inspiration in the *Pensées* of Pascal. We may credit Maistre with having seen the dependence of theology upon religion and with having recognized the authority of Pascal on the role of religion in the life of the mind. As a body of doctrinal thought, traditionalism comes to a close in the works of Lamennais. At its best, however, perhaps in the *Soirées de Saint-Pétersbourg*, it represents a sincere attempt to bring the religious conviction and ethical clarity of the seventeenth century into the more perplexed and subtle currents of the Romantic period.

FELICITE DE LAMENNAIS (1782-1854)

Between 1800 and 1830 the traditionalist movement gained prestige from the popularity of Chateaubriand, Lamartine and the neo-Christian literary successes. At the same time its doctrines emerged with sharper definition. The advent of Hugo and Lamennais in the 1820's promised to consolidate the first triumphs of unified, modern Christian thought over popular imagination. Lamennais in particular gives finality to the traditionalist position affirming the unique powers of the Catholic Church as a unifying social force. In 1825 the *Mémorial Catholique* announced that "Christianity, in general, is the strongest and in fact the only strong political society, because Christianity is the truest and only true religious society" (Tome III, p. 330). So, contrary to the eighteenth-century political philosopher who saw in church and state a monolithic system of autocracy and oppression, the nineteenth-century traditionalist saw in retrospect the evils of revolution and attributed these evils to the weakness of a state which had not acquired a firm enough foundation within the structure of Christianity.

Bonald and Maistre had attacked the divisive movements such as Protestantism and rationalism, which had broken up the great Christian hegemonies of Europe. Yet even the Catholic world was not committed to policies of total social cohesion under the Church. One of the chief documents formulating the relationship of church and state was the Declaration of Four Articles of 1682, which recognized

47

the complete independence of royal authority in the affairs of state and the priority of ecumenical councils over the Pope in the determination of doctrine. The goals of traditionalism therefore became: the revival of Christian faith among the mass of believers who had been carried away with revolutionary enthusiasms, the restoration of authoritative government directly subject to the spiritual authority of Rome and a centralized source of Christian doctrine in the Pope. Neither Bonald nor Maistre recognized in the revolutionary spirit an evolution in society's concept of itself, and the Abbé Félicité de Lamennais may be considered both a pioneer of the "social Gospel" and a victim of the attempt to bring this new social consciousness under the sanction of Christian institutions. We shall conclude our study of traditionalism with an analysis of Lamennais' revolt from the original position of Bonald and Maistre and the role of Pascal in the final scenes of this movement in France.

* * *

PASCAL AND THE *ESSAY ON INDIFFERENCE*. A casual glance shows that Lamennais composed much of the *Essay* under the inspiration of Pascal, Bossuet, Bonald and Maistre. It has been suggested that he owed his Christian convictions to the "wager" of Pascal, and Amoudru concludes: "At least it is established that he read and meditated the writings of his uncle Saudrais, where the philosophers who could 'take up and penetrate' the most important questions are refuted with the aid of Pascal. Several of the hundred thoughts forming the continuation of the *Bon Curé* are borrowed from Pascal. Abbé Jean provides extracts from the *Pensées*."[1] The influence of Pascal is evident in the very title of Lamennais' work, as the first page of the Port-Royal edition bears the title: *against indifference*. The 1817 edition of the *Essay* opens and closes with quotations from Pascal, and the author wrote to his brother in the same year: "Pascal's work should reappear almost in its entirety in mine, and furnish nearly half the content."

The introduction to the first edition is Pascalian both in style and in spirit. There is the same ironic recreation of the human condition, the same urgent dissatisfaction with spiritual lethargy: "Only

48

glance for a moment at this king of creation: what incomprehensible slavishness! His sluggish mind is content with shadows. Ignorance is his joy, his peace, his felicity; he has lost even his desire to know that which concerns him the most. . ." (*Essay*, 1, 4) The formal duality of human nature arises once more as an inescapable product of original sin, and the heart is identified as the moral stimulus in the quest for ultimate truth: "Inconsistency torments the human heart as much as it revolts reason; and for this reason it often suffices to change one's mode of living to believe the truth which one had been denying. . . . Error produces false enthusiasms, indifference lulls the mind; but neither can sustain the hungry heart" (*Essay*, 1, pp. 10 and 28). But for Lamennais the heart is never more than an inward capacity for conviction. It arouses the sense of moral obligation which gives man the assurance of causality in his attempt to bring about the good in the concrete world of struggle and conflict. Still, Lamennais' concern is for the general social fabric rather than the individual. We shall see how intimately the Christian ethic is linked in the mind of Lamennais with social action.

The main body of the *Essay* attacks three doctrines which, according to Lamennais, lead to self-contradiction and indifference: atheism, which would place truth in the state itself; the natural religion of Rousseau and the English deists, which leads to the imposition of state over church, and Protestantism, whose interpretations of the Bible leave belief at the mercy of reason. The author's method consists of demonstrating that all doctrines using reason as a primary instrument must fall into all the excesses of which human reason is capable. Truth must be essentially One, and all systems which produce a diversity of opinion must be false and lead to doubt. The true basis of belief must be sought elsewhere. We shall follow the process by which Lamennais turns from the personally experienced faith of Pascal in search of a faith capable of transforming the very nature of society.

* * *

REASON AND SOCIAL THEORY. We have observed that Lamennais quotes Pascal on the subject of original sin, and refers to

49

the theme once or twice elsewhere. For Pascal, the fall from grace deprived man of the rational responses upon which an orderly society must be founded. The *Pensées* sowed in the mind of Lamennais a few doubts which never troubled the systematic serenity of Bonald: "The art of overthrowing states, as Pascal said so well, lies in disturbing established customs by tracing them to their sources . . . It is a game which can only bring defeat. Nothing resists rational analysis, and society less than all the rest." (*Essay* 1, p.261). But the earliest form of Lamennais' political theory is thoroughly impregnated with traditionalism. Since man does not contain within himself the potential seeds of social order, he must submit to a political system based upon an imposed order. With Bonald, Lamennais finds a necessary, although exterior, morality in the hierarchical form of government:

> For there is no social order without a social hierarchy, without power and without subjects, without the right to command and the duty to obey. Now between equal beings there can of course be neither duties nor rights . . . and society will never be built with men alone: man must first be in society with God in order to be able to enter into relationship with God, before entering into society with his fellow beings.[2]

Evidence of political morality therefore lies in the capacity of government to unify the Christian community. It is on this basis that Lamennais is to judge the reigns of Charles X and Louis-Philippe and to find in the narrowness of their vision reasons for rejecting the phase of traditionalism which would link the fate of Catholicism with that of monarchy.

Lamennais does refer on one occasion to the analogy between monarchy and the "necessary hierarchy" of society, but it is significant that on the whole he does not insist upon any privileged form of temporal government. Universal authority can come from God alone and be expressed only in the spiritual institution established by Him. More rigorous a logician than Bonald, Lamennais translates his feeling for the unity of truth into a strict theocracy: no stable society other than that which draws its authority from the true religion, no true religion outside of Christianity, no Christianity without its visible manifestation in the Church and no Church without the Pope.[3] We shall find the complete expression of this theme in the *Avenir* and its culmination in the papal encyclical *Mirari vos* drawn up against it in 1832. But perhaps what distinguishes Lamennais most decisively from the traditional apologists for Christianity is his search for a tangible basis of belief derived from the universal forms of society, rather than the supernatural forms of revealed religion.

In our study of Bonald, we noted that Pascal held that Christianity embodied a superior truth which presided over the relative truths, or traditional customs, of the different cultures of man, and that the essence of this superior truth was accessible only to faith and converted into moral action through the disposition of the "heart." Consequently there would be an adequate basis for man's acceptance of the culture in which he must fulfil his temporal existence, but one necessarily conditioned by the experience of Christian religion. With Pascal, Lamennais denies the capacity of individual reason to produce any valid criterion of truth. Instead of placing the focal point of belief in the heart of the individual, however, he extends it to embrace the universal expression of human reason in the *consensus gentium,* or general truths of society.

The assumption underlying the philosophical doctrine of common consent is that individual reason is like a single cell of a many-celled animal. It cannot in itself comprehend the purpose of the entire organism, but is nevertheless bound by the laws governing the whole. The appeal of Lamennais' argument in his own day may be found in two factors. In the first place, it is consonant with the tenets of eclecticism, although Lamennais would have objected to the analogy, to assume that the basic beliefs of philosophic systems in general concerning the true nature of man may be combined to give a more universal picture of truth than any single system. In a theological sense, this would apply to the separate systems of religion. Unlike the eclectics, however, Lamennais presupposes the universality of Christianity which was imperfectly prefigured in primitive religions. His efforts to prove the monotheistic nature of all pre-Christian religions attracted the attention of the political and religious syncretists, but exposed him to the opposition of all "free-thinking" anthropologists. The second source of power in the *Essay* is more a matter of methodology. Like Pascal, Lamennais would require individual human reason to recognize the absolute necessity of committing itself to some more encompassing mode of being, forcing the issue on man's incapacity to achieve the truth in himself while demonstrating the impossibility of renouncing truth as his ultimate goal:

> But if we do not suppose human reason infallible, there is no other basis for certitude; and to be consistent, we would have to doubt everything. Now, whatever efforts he may make to arrive at this state of doubting, man is completely incapable of succeeding. His whole nature resists invincibly. He would destroy himself rather than relinquish his belief. Therefore nature forces him either to live in perpetual contradiction with reason or to admit the infallibility of human reason or the reason of all men.[4]

In the second volume of the *Essay*, appearing in 1820, Lamennais sought to elaborate the dependence of man upon society for any degree of certainty. He had intended to develop in subsequent volumes the way in which revealed truth is preserved through tradition and embodied in the doctrines of the Catholic church. With a human, universal criterion of truth, directly attached to the teachings of the church, young Catholic intellectuals might well feel that in Lamennais they had found the spearhead of a rejuvenated and unified Christian Europe. Opposition to the new movement arose from so many directions, however, that the author of the *Essay* was obliged for a time to undertake the defense of his position in the journalistic arena.

When Pascal attacked the pretensions of human reason, it was for the purpose of demonstrating the existence of an intuitive form of cognition capable of modifying one's mode of being in a more essential way than intellection ... Lamennais, on the other hand, has denied to individual reason what he would accord to universal reason and has replaced Pascal's appeal to the religious instinct with an authoritarian concept of society rigidly molded within the Catholic hierarchy. The Jansenist *Chronique religieuse* is one of the first to point out the absence of a religious motivation in the new philosophy:

> What is the objective of these assertions that the sense of true and false, of good and evil, as variable as our ideas, depends upon education and prejudices; that, like thought, it is the result of

society; that religion has no foundation within ourselves; that these words: *religious thought, religious feeling* express no more than vague reveries of the heart . . . . ?[5]

Lamennais' reply in the *Drapeau blanc* takes the form of a bitter diatribe on the voices of moderation and compromise which have weakened the integrity of the church as a leader of societies. By 1823 his ardor has reached such a peak that the *Constitutionnel* sees in him the avenging shade of Torquemada.

*   *   *

CHRISTIAN POLEMICS. Within the church itself hostility to the Mennaisian doctrine was strong and outspoken. The successor of Bonald and Maistre represents the Ultramontanist party against the majority of the Bishops of France, who, as Gallicans would safeguard the rights and privileges of the French clergy in the Catholic hierarchy. Indeed, Lamennais became the voice of ultramontanism. With his appeal to Rome to declare its leadership as the only source of political and social morality, he attracted many minds eager for reform and for a purified chain of authority within the church. It is small wonder that all the established forces of Catholicism, Jesuits, Jansenists and Gallicans should view such proposals with alarm. Moreover, Lamennais had set his seal upon the Catholic church *visible* as the only true expression of the beliefs and the will of God. By entering into the nineteenth century as a social force, the church might have become a determining factor in the social revolution, but at the cost of setting aside its religious character. In any case, Rome remained silent for the time being, forcing Lamennais to assume the responsibility for his attempt to apply Catholicism to the diseases of society. By the time he learns that the church is unwilling to champion the cause for which he stands, he has reached a point of commitment from which he can withdraw only by betraying his cause or his church.

It would be interesting to follow the Battle of the Journals between Gallicans, Ultramontanists, Jansenists, Jesuits, Protestants, Moralists and Philanthropists during this second decade of the century, including Lamennais' trip to Rome with Gerbet and Lacordaire

53

in a fruitless attempt to win a definitive pronouncement from Pope Leo XII. There is enough material for a chapter on the use of Pascal in polemic literature of the period. Emotions are too troubled, however, for serious reflection upon the deeper meanings of the *Pensées*, and many of the quotations are only of momentary interest, as when Lamennais accuses the Gallicans of being governed by private concerns instead of submission to ecclesiastical authority:

> A secret principle of revolt, hidden deep within the human heart, and which even virtue cannot eradicate completely, struggles persistently within us against everything which seems to menace our independence. They submit as little as possible, and as *the will*, according to the profound comment of Pascal, *is one of the principal organs of belief*, it inclines the mind to whatever is pleasing to it . . . So great is the weakness of man, that he will reject the manifest truth, not for any powerful motive, not through violent hatred, but for a reason often so petty, that he is scarcely conscious of it; . . . . and nevertheless the truth is God![6]

Pascal emerged from the polemic hostilities of the *Provincial Letters* with a more certain faith capable of providing measure and control to the religious experience which unified the *Pensées*. Lamennais on the contrary has been drawn both intellectually and emotionally to concentrate upon the present welfare of society, the love for mankind which is so consuming that it will never permit him to divorce himself from the historical struggles of his day in search of transcendent principles. The final epoch of traditionalism swings completely away from the dogmatic spirit in which it was conceived, and we shall conclude this phase of our study with a brief analysis of the implications of this neo-Christian sociology.

The social orientation of Christian thought is slowly established in the tentative program of the *Avenir*, from 1830-1831. Pascal still retains an honorary position of influence in the new conception of the relationship of religion to society. For Lamennais there is still an essential difference between the relative laws of culture and the general laws of man's religious origins:

> If private interests can momentarily bring men together, the knot which joins them should, to borrow the expression of Pascal, take its *loops and folds* from something much more profound, which

touches the most intimate and noble forms of their nature. This bond of the spirit, this law which, while controlling thoughts and wills, introduces the individual into a unified society, is what all people call religion.[7]

Yet in the following year it becomes evident that the future to which the *Avenir* is dedicated both in name and spirit is to be brought about in the concentrated heart of society rather than the tormented heart of the individual: "The temporal royalty of Christ, by the freeing of the people and liberty of thought and conscience, the absolute separation, in their respective jurisdictions, of Church and State, of the spiritual and administrative orders: that is the goal of Christian society, that is what will be."[8] The notion of universal consent has thus led Lamennais to identify Catholicism so closely with liberal social action that the silence of Rome during the persecution of the faithful in Poland in 1832 appeared, in his eyes, a criminal act and contrary to the very spirit of the universal church. A final trip to Rome in the summer of 1832 demonstrated the antipathy of Gregory XVI to the social goals set forth in the *Avenir*. In his encyclical *Mirari vos,* the Pope condemned the doctrines of freedom of conscience and of the press and silenced those who would bring about the separation of church and state. The submission of Lamennais and his decision to dissolve the *Avenir* have caused many critics to set a later date for his break with the Catholic church, but we have seen in his original interpretation that Lamennais was never so submissive to the Catholic church as to an idealized Christian organization capable of performng a miraculous cohesion of the hostile elements of nineteenth-century society.

* * *

FAITH OF THE REBEL. The Memorial which Pascal carried in his heart after 1654 did not prevent the storm of controversy from breaking upon him, but certainly contributed to the steadfastness with which he defended the intuitive realities of Christianity. It would be no distortion to consider Lamennais' *Paroles d'un croyant* as a sort of Memorial, a personal rededication of the gospels to the suffering masses caught between two revolutions. The tone of this work is inspired and prophetic, permeated with a longing for the introduction of Christian doctrines into the kingdoms of men: "A great battle will be fought, and the angel of justice and the angel of love will unite with those who struggle to establish among men the reign of justice and the rule of love."[9] The *Paroles d'un croyant* stand as an isolated attempt to inject a religious dimension into the rationalistic and materialistic current of political thought extending from Rousseau's vision of the *demos* to Marx's "reign of the proletariat." In the *Affaires de Rome*, in 1836, Lamennais announces that he has abandoned the "Christianity of the pontificate" for a "Christianity of the human race," and from this moment he is to know all the isolation, persecutions and even physical imprisonment of the social reformer without a party. History was forcing him to chose between his love for the masses and his allegiance to the institutions of Christianity. His only support is a constant faith in the collective capacity of mankind to fulfil the promise of Christian doctrine.

The most complete statement of the position to which Lamennais' thinking has evolved appears in his *Esquisse d'une philosophie*, a work which is generally overlooked because of the more dramatic aspects of the author's public struggle with the authorities of church and state. The treatise represents an attempted synthesis of philosophy and religious positivism, in which reason would be restored as an instrument of religious understanding. The section which is most pertinent to this study, however, is the definition of human nature in terms of metaphysical chain-of-being and the refutation of original sin, with Pascal a chosen adversary. There is a visual clarity and refinement of expression in the *Esquisse* which places it above most of the philosophical productions of the Romantic period and certainly merits this brief, concluding analysis.

Although we have observed that Lamennais skirted the problem of evil in the *Essay on Indifference*, it is nevertheless true that he accepted the doctrine, and even incorporated it into the *Paroles d'un croyant*. The exposition of human suffering in the *Esquisse d'une philosophie* recalls much of the imagery and sensitivity to psychological conflict with which Pascal approached the question:

A profound disorder exists therefore at the roots of human nature. Man is not what he should be. Sorry combination of contrasting elements, he undoubtedly shows impressive signs of greatness, but a greatness which is obscure, dissipated and incomplete. King of the earth, he can change its surface, overcoming its blind forces by a superior force whose principle lies within him, yet his feeble existence is the plaything of his environment. He suffers, trembles and fears; boredom, disgust, anguish, have become the characteristics of his life, and complaint his natural speech. Frightful mystery! and who can explain it? Evil is in the world.[10]

More and more drawn to Leibniz, Lamennais refuses to admit a distinct category to evil. What man experiences of evil is rather a temporary sense of the isolation of an organic entity which will inevitably be discarded as soon as man discovers the higher processes of unification with his fellow men and with God. Evil exists therefore only for the individual and not for the species. The doctrine of the fall from grace is false, since it presents sin as an inheritance of the perverted will, although the will, according to Lamennais, is a part of man's spiritual individuality, and therefore not transmissible in the same way that disease may be inherited through organic continuity of the species. Indeed, the incomplete nature of man is a first step in the divine law of progress, by which he recognizes that, alone, he has been something less, and that in conjunction with society and God he may become something more. Much of this doctrine appeared in the social ideologies of the era which we are observing, from Ballanche through the Saint-Simonists and Fourierists to Leroux and Reynaud. It represents a logical, rather than psychological, demonstration of the goodness of God, and an almost mystical faith in the destiny of mankind. For Lamennais, it served as the uncompromising ideal underlying his political activity as a member of the Constitutional Committee during the early days of the Second Republic, and as a spiritual guarantee of the complete integrity with which he maintained his liberal convictions in spite of the increasing isolation and hostility which oppressed his final years.

Outward similarities between the histories of Pascal and Jansenism and Lamennais and Ultramontanism have led to much speculation on the attitude which Pascal would have taken, had he been forced to face the decisions of the recipient of the condemnatory encyclical

Singulari nos. Both men appear in the history of ideas as apologists for Christianity, but at the same time as authors of polemics creating broad divisions within the church. In 1836 Alexandre Vinet suggests that there is an essential distinction between the religious positon of Lamennais and that of Pascal as both seek to resolve their common scepticism. Referring to the attack which both led against the validity of individual reason, Vinet concludes that Pascal "has only pretended to accuse the helplessness of reason and nature in the matter of religion; but instead of directing us, like Lamennais, to the Church, he has referred us to the Holy Spirit."[11] Yet it is certain that the orthodoxy of Pascal was as troubled by the signature of retraction of the Jansenistic articles as that of Lamennais by the acts of submission to which he was required to affix his name. How would Pascal have responded to the excommunications which met the doctrines of Lamennais? Giraud considers this question of ultimate allegiance in his suggestion that "if it is true that there was in Pascal the makings of a great heretic, can we compare him to Lamennais? In any case, he would not have created a schism for the same reasons, since Lamennais left the Church for *social* purposes, while Pascal was impelled by motives drawn from his ardent need for 'inner life' . . ."[12] We would perhaps be more just if we set aside the historical comparison of men and doctrines, and recognized in both Pascal and Lamennais a generous capacity for humility and submissiveness. The inevitable distinction between the two authors would then appear in the aspect of Christianity which for each constituted authority. For Pascal, the core of Christianity furnishes a stable foundation for the permanent residence of an otherwise transient self, while for Lamennais, it is the essence of the entire social fabric. The twentieth century has partially vindicated Lamennais by the centralization of authority in the Catholic Church and the elaboration of a Christian social doctrine. The *Pensées* are now regarded as a classic in Christian apology, and continue to maintain the validity of the religious experience as an integral part of the human psyche in the attitudes of modern phychologists.

George Boas, in his *French Philosophies of the Romantic Period*, is critical of the "wasted energies" consumed by the traditionalist movement in an attempt to reform society under the auspices of a

Christian organization which eventually disavowed their most sincere efforts. A general condemnation of the abortive schools of nineteenth-century thought is mitigated, however, by the author's conclusion that: "A real history of ideas ought to see that the importance of a thought is to be measured by the stimulus which calls it forth."[18] If we consider the total stimulus to which the traditionalists were responding, we shall understand the magnitude of their task. From Pascal, Malebranche, Leibniz and Bossuet they received a challenge to keep alive in French culture the keenest sense of God's will and creative action permeating the forms of human understanding and assuring a permanent source of inspiration for man as a moral agent. From the eighteenth century came an equally impelling challenge to realize the full potential of the individual considered as a rational whole by means of a social evolution which would replace conventional stability and authority with a free selectivity modeled on nature. To increase the difficulties of nineteenth-century philosophy, it was generally assumed that these two currents of thought were mutually exclusive, that Christianity was socially repressive and that popular democracy was somehow atheistic. To a considerable extent traditionalism may be said to have demonstrated the possibility of the coexistence of these two fundamental, but conflicting, visions of reality.

Although traditionalism is introduced by Bonald as a conservative social doctrine destined to replace rationalism with Catholic theology, there is a distinct change of emphasis under Maistre and Lamennais, transferring the criterion of authority from the arbitrary claims of cult to a more philosophical view based upon the social and ethical nature of man. It is in this turning point of the traditionalist movement that the influence of Pascal is most clearly seen. As Maistre searches below the surface of human conventions for an intuitive, universal characteristic of moral action, he finds in Pascal's "Christianity of the heart" a deeper and more personal source of unity than that attaching to any of the systems of man. The same liberating and unifying action is to be found in Lamennais' relationship with Pascal in the *Essay on Indifference*. The definition of man's contingency, his desire for certainty and his struggle to achieve fulfilment on broader levels of being are derived in large part from the *Pensées*. Although he has found in Christian liberalism a satisfactory goal for moral life, and in universal reason a refuge from intellectual uncertainty, Lamennais has succeeded in preserving both the metaphysical and social aspirations of his predecessors.

The social revolution presented an accomplished fact which nineteenth-century philosophy was called upon to organize into a comprehensible pattern, and it is not the least contribution of the traditionalists to this task to have defined the approach to the problem of human motivation with a concern for ethical consistency clearly derived from Pascal. The movement set out to establish the authority of religion in the creation of a more perfect society, and discovered in Pascal an authority on the religious experience capable of girding up the loftiest structures which sociology could conceive. The vision of Lamennais is secularized in the "religion of humanity" of Auguste Comte. The reforms for which he struggled are outlined in the encyclical *Rerum Novarum*, in 1891, when Leo XIII declared: "That some remedy must be found, and found quickly, for the misery and wretchedness pressing so heavily and unjustly at this moment on the vast majority of the working classes."[14] It is this encyclical which Pius indicated as the origin of "a true Catholic social science." We have seen the crucible from which this science was cast: the traditionalist movement of ideas.

Early Romantic Writers

In 1752 an English anthologist of French literary thought presented a collection of anecdotes relating the successes of Pascal over the atheists and Epicureans of his day. The author observed with scholarly interest that: "All the imperfect scraps of paper which were found to contain any of Pascal's *Thoughts,* have been pasted on so many sheets of fine paper, and very richly bound into one book, which is kept in a public library at Paris, and shown to curious strangers, as a most valuable curiosity."[1] Within the next decade a number of French writers were born who transformed the object of curiosity into one of the most revered landmarks of modern thought. Between the generation Restif de la Bretonne and the Marquis de Sade and that of Lamartine, Musset, Vigny and Hugo there are voices preparing the way for a new vision of man, based on a new-found tradition. With the flaming careers of Danton, Robespierre and Napoleon there also came into existence the healers and visionaries, the poets of peace, Charles-Julien de Chênedollé, Pierre-Simon Ballanche and François-René de Chateaubriand. Each of these representatives of early romanticism has contributed to the creation of an esthetic synthesis of the self in its relationship to nature and God which carried over into the symbolism of the last half of the century. Not the least of their achievements was their conversion of Pascal from the reputed gloomy moralist into a guiding spirit of religious imagination.

During the formative years of romanticism Bonald, Maistre and Lamennais struggled to bring forth the Catholic Church militant and triumphant. As ultra-conservatives, their influence was limited to the political sphere. They were identified with monarchy and ultramontanism and when the Church itself repudiated the direction of their thought, Lamennais continued to pursue the phantom of perfectibility through institution. The early Romantics mentioned above

61

were also looking for a spiritual revival, but with less rigid conceptions of a final truth and a greater range of intellectual origins. They
were poets with a profound sense of history. They were men of
gentleness and moderation who were appalled by the Jacobin terror,
but who would not yield to a Restoration which refused to assume
the responsibilities of a free society. They have been frequently overlooked in favor of the more exaggerated figures of their times, but
critics in the twentieth century have been steadily increasing our
understanding of their contributions to the evolution of Western
culture.

Chênedollé, Ballanche and Chateaubriand devoted their lives to
the preservation and revitalization of the French literary heritage.
They looked beyond Racine and Boileau for esthetic inspiration which
would loosen the creative energies of French Romanticism. They discovered in Plato the sources of a new idealism and in Saint Augustine
the personal account of religious faith achieved in anguish and in a
world of turmoil. They turned from the great rational systems of
Aristotle and Saint Thomas and consulted the mystics and the moralists. Their influence was felt in circles where the new and significant literature was being formed. Their friendships included Restif
de la Bretonne and Fontanes, Grand Master of the University, but
their most intimate contributions were stimulated by the presence of
the charming and wonderful Mme Récamier, Mme de Beaumont,
Mme d'Hautefeuille and Mme Swetchine.[2] They corresponded with
Mme de Staël, Musset, Vigny, Hugo, Lamartine and Sainte-Beuve.
Their feeling for the past and their response to the present provided
the atmosphere in which the romantic movement was nourished. In
a way they show the full evolution of that peculiar mixture of erudition, artistry and prophetic insight which was extinguished on the
guillotine with André Chénier.

* * *

PASCAL AND THE ROMANTIC COMPLEX. The eclectic philosophy of the early Romantics laid pitfalls from which not all of
them escaped. Sensitive to the most diverse inspirations of the past,
they frequently dissipated their energies in broad panoramas with no

point of focus at which the eye might stop to discover the meaning of the particular and its relation to the whole. Charles-Julien de Chênedollé (1769-1833) represents one of those literary figures whose poetic imagination failed to fuse the grandiose visions of society, religion and reason which flowed from his pen. In his long, didactic poem, the *Génie de l'homme* (1807), Chênedollé adopts a form which was used by Pope and Delille and which continues to tempt Lamartine, Musset, Vigny, Hugo and Sully-Prud'homme in the nineteenth century. The poem attempts to convert into poetic images a broad philosophical and religious treatise on the origins, nature and purposes of man. Such a vast project requires either the lively convictions of a Pope or the powerful rhythms of a Lamartine if it is to seize and hold the reader's attention. Chênedollé does not quite succeed. Of course he contends that poetry does not seek to create ideas: "It merely proposes to popularize them and propose them for public admiration." So he must be judged by the elements of the past which he wishes to popularize and the ideas which he admires.

In view of his conception of the critical role of poetry, Chênedollé's reverence for Pascal is particularly significant: "There are men whose intelligence is so complete that one might call them spherical geniuses. Such is Pascal."[3] In the contest between Rousseau and Pascal for the imagination of the Romantics, Chêndollé suggests that the latter is more transcendent: "He takes you brusquely by the hair and draws you to heaven." After Louis Racine's attempt in *De la religion* to versify the thoughts of Pascal and Bossuet, Chêndollé decides to illuminate Pascal by presenting his ideas among the latest discoveries in science and sociology. The third *Chant,* intended to enhance the prestige of Pascal, is concerned with human psychology: "It is Man who observes and descends within himself." The self which is discovered is a Pascalian one—a chimera, glorious and miserable at the same time. The stylistic effect unfortunately reminds us that there are certain ramparts which cannot be stormed by the muse: imagine if you can a lyric rendition of the Ten Commandments. Pascal's vigor comes from his vivid sense of contrast: "Man is but a reed, the weakest in nature; but he is a thinking reed." Chênedollé softens the contours with a metaphorical style which emerges as a series of flat epithets and man is defined as an "Ambitious insect, frail and thinking reed."

The climax of this *Chant* introduces Pascal to the heart of the Romantic spirit. Chênedollé reviews the problem of evil and ends by reproducing the misery-greatness paradox of Pascal:

> Fortune! What have I said? This fickle goal
> That man pursues to seize and have it whole, ...
> Pure happiness on earth cannot be found,
> From good to evil there's an endless round.[4]

He observes the transience of passion and worldly success, but instead of attempting to identify the true nature of such a world he weighs its poetic depth. So Pascal's conclusions concerning the religious quality of life are transformed into the cult of poetic genius:

> So true it is that Man by talents chained
> On earth a passerby, sublime but maimed,
> Cannot without misfortune end a life
> Which Heaven's gift of genius turned to strife.

Just as Chateaubriand's apology for Christianity orchestrates the theme of the solitary, passionate soul in *René*, so Pascal's apology is transformed in the third *Chant* into poetic material for Léon, Chênedollé's René. A Romantic Pascal is thus fixed in its theoretic aspect and converted into the melancholic image of an "enfant du siècle."

* * *

PASCAL AND THE ROMANTIC POETS. The value of Pascal's incisive descriptions and his "heroic" confrontation of life in its tragic aspect is not lost on Lamartine or Vigny. It is well known that Lamartine's "Eternité de la nature" in the *Harmonies poétiques* constitutes an extended version of Pascal's *pensée* of the "thinking reed." The same theme recurs throughout the *Harmonies,* appearing in the most concise form in "l'Humanité":

> A man! a son, a king of nature's might!
> An insect born of mud, who lives on light!
> Who fills but a point, who has a moment's grace,
> But who can master endless worlds in thought
> And, ever forcing back the limits wrought,
> Extends his being through all time and space.

Throughout his religious poetry before 1835 Lamartine makes use of Pascalian images. The abyss of doubt, the impassive silence of nature reappear, but in a context which blends them into a sort of lullaby. For Lamartine it is sweet to float "between doubt and hope." The silence of nature has no finality: inevitably it gives way to the light of dawn and consolation. Lamartine of course will never grasp the thrust from despair to desire in Pascal's thirst for the infinite. For him the heart is an end in itself rather than an instrument for touching the thickly-veiled face of God. The sense of infinity "opens marvelous perspectives to the imagination, incites thought and stimulates the heart by sublime aspirations."[5] But the option is never forced, as James would say, and the experience is never more than "poetic." Only in Hugo's "gulfs" and "abysses" or in Vigny's hidden God do we find vibrant and full responses to the challenge of Pascal.

The problem of the intellectual romantics like Vigny and Hugo is one of finding a faith which would provide either a gnostic certainty of the nature of God or a complete revelation of the meaning of human suffering. Like the rationalist, they want to heal the wounds of man; as moralists and visionaries they seek total intuitions of truth. A sensitive study by Charles Hill shows the way in which this divine discontent in Vigny leads to a life-long struggle with Pascal. The creation by the Romantics of a Pascal haunted by doubt revealed a deep level of moral and intellectual anguish pervading the modern mind. Vigny's *Journal* reveals a mind in which love aroused deep desires for God and yet which intellectual and moral firmness prevented from easy consolations. Hill concludes that "Vigny was a believer to the extent that Pascal was a doubter; the latter's doubt was as real as his belief, as real as Christ's anguish in 'Le mystère de Jésus.' If Vigny was basically a doubter, he experienced Jesus' belief in 'Le mont des Oliviers.' "[6] Critics of the Romantic poets point to their inability to displace themselves from the center of the stage, showing an immaturity and excessive egoism. On the other hand, there is evidence in the works of all these poets that in part they have assumed the burden of doubt for their generation and that their refusal to displace themselves from the central action constitutes a sincere attempt to measure the frightening limits of the human condition within the arena of their own hearts. The integrity of their quest is revealed in their constant and personal responses to the metaphysical questions of human dignity raised by Pascal.

PIERRE-SIMON BALLANCHE (1776-1847) witnessed the wastefulness in human lives of the Terror as it struck Lyon during his youth. His compassionate nature led him to look to religion for a social philosophy, some new interpretation of the divine plan, which would guide men to peaceful evolution rather than revolution. His first book, *Du Sentiment dans ses rapports avec la littérature et les arts* (1801), reveals the meditations of a sensitive nature on themes which were to become the commonplaces of Romanticism: the charms of the country, the nature of melancholy, the esthetic values of religion. Although the discontinuity of his thought and the heaviness of his erudition were severely dealt with by the critics, Ballanche is generally credited with the creation of a new source of literary inspiration. Among many curious analogies between this work and the *Génie du christianisme* of Chateaubriand is the fact that Chateaubriand's title is found in the *Du Sentiment*. These similarities as well as the freshness of Ballanche's religious thought give him a rightful place as one of the founding fathers of Romanticism.

Another strange coincidence between the two works occurs in their references to Pascal. Ballanche wrote that "a line of Pascal (is) as sacred for us as . . . an ancient column standing on the ruins of Palmyra or Babylon." At almost the same moment Chateaubriand was saying of the *Pensées*: "It is like seeing the ruins of Palmyra, superb remnants of genius and time . . . " In view of Ballanche's lifelong concern with the *Pensées*, it is surprising that so little has been said of the results of this relationship. Rastoul shows that Ballanche's debut as a journalist, the twelfth of brumaire in the year XIII, was with a Fragment on the *Penseés* inserted in the *Bulletin de Lyon*. George notes that during the 1840's Ballanche was anxious to fan the flames of what he considered to be the sparks of a Catholic revival and that to this end he intensified his studies of Pascal: "He felt an affinity for Pascal, the religious writer and the inventor. Both had fought the good fight for a world in which spiritual values might prevail; both had desired the establishment of a real Christian ethics."[7]

Much of his early writing seems to have been composed with

Pascal close at hand. It is interesting to observe how the gentle mystic of Lyons interprets the public and private tragedies which he had experienced through the perspective of the sixteenth-century moralist. Pascal said: "The last act is bloody, however beautiful the play: they throw some dirt on the head and that's that forever (Br. p.428)." Pierre-Simon reflects on the massacres at Lyons and writes: "The just man is oppressed and a shovelfull of earth thrown over him ends his misery; the wicked triumphs and a shovelfull of earth thrown over him ends his triumph . . . Where then is the goal? Prideful man! Be like Pascal, throw yourself in the dust and confess your nothingness." The unhappy conclusion of his courtship of Bertille d'Avèze apparently leads him to ponder the *pensées* on the "misery of man." In opposition to the great rationalist systems Pascal contended that "Man is but a subject of error." In his early gropings for love and waverings between a life of religion or the world, Ballanche has known the confusions of both heart and mind: "How much man is subject to error! He never knows what he wants nor what he desires. He is mistaken about the most intimate things of his heart . . . Perhaps he should even beware of the counsels of virtue, so great is his misery and so ignorant is he of what is good."[8]

Chateaubriand is generally credited with the creation of a "Romantic Pascal" and undoubtedly the portrait which he drew in the *Gënie du christianisme* imposed itself on the minds of his contemporaries. The picture which Ballanche is composing at much the same time is no less striking and contains many of the elements which appealed to Chateaubriand. "This man whom we see at the edge of the grave, still young and meditating on eternity, casts our souls into the deep thoughts of solitude and reveals to our heart all the wonders of religion." Here is what Pascal represented to the new man of the nineteenth century: a solitary genius brooding on his hidden God, a man of suffering and integrity who came to understand the human heart through his religion. These images and attitudes occur with such spontaneity in the works of Lamartine, Vigny and the other romantics that one is ready to believe in some spiritual fraternity of the intellect. Quite naturally the picture which the Romantic artist paints of Pascal is that of a René in whom the will is miraculously preserved from the "mal de siècle," but who understands the nature of that illness.

This disciple of Pascal, however, is also fascinated by the attempt to understand individual man in terms of the evolution of society and, as a concomitant, the problem of evil. In the works of his maturity, the *Essai sur les institutions sociales*, the *Essais de palingénésie sociale* and the *Ville des expiations*, Ballanche develops a vision of the collective fate of humanity. While remaining within the Catholic tradition, he introduces the secular utopic movements of Fourier, Saint-Simon, Pierre Leroux and Jean Reynaud to the point that the Saint-Simonist leader Enfantin wrote the rather unwelcome news that only they "will understand the regenerative idea of the Palingenesis and will sympathize with it." The peculiar fate of Ballanche's works may be explained in part by the fact that his notion that social evolution was destined to bring about the triumph of plebians over patricians did not please conservative Catholic circles, while his Christian orthodoxy repelled the founders of the new social order.

The problem which Ballanche was trying to identify for his times was a familiar one to Christian thinkers: "What is the relationship of human society to the design of Providence?" For Saint Augustine and for Dante there is a single dispensation for the citizens of the Empire and those of the Church. The laws of society form a distinct pattern in the divine plan, but one which parallels that of the spiritual kingdom. So the civil criminal is subject to spiritual punishment, and Brutus and Judas come together under the jaws of Pluto. Pascal considers society to be the product of human invention alone, bearing only indirectly the marks of a divine origin in the mixture of sublimity and depravity of its citizens. There is consequently for Pascal no political institution which contains an inherent legitimacy, while apocalyptic visions of the rise or fall of mankind remain veiled to him in a mystery far too deep to penetrate. In the nineteenth century the question is again raised by visionaries. Ballanche would combine the personal ethics of Pascal with some dream for humanity which would justify through religion the social salvation which the Enlightenment had failed to acquire through reason.

Pascal has made distinct impressions on the sociology of Ballanche. In his Fragment on Justice, Pascal supposed that man would never attain an ultimate social truth: "Raise the curtain. It is in vain, whether we must believe or deny or doubt..." The basis of his conclusion is that there can be no such ultimate truth since human existence is finite. Ballanche seems to follow Pascal's political relativism: "Social doctrines can never be completely revealed. The statue of Isis was covered with a triple veil: the first was lifted by the neophytes, the second by the sanctuary priests; but the third was sacred for all." Social truth and justice are therefore the same for Ballanche as religious truth, a mystery buried in the roots of creation. Unlike the mysteries of religion, however, the secrets of man's origin and final end serve for Ballanche as a challenge to poetic imagination and his purpose becomes one of seeking the great synthesis of religion and sociology.

Even here Ballanche strains Pascalian notions to bring them into conformity with his social idealism. Much of the *Institutions sociales* seems to have been written with Pascal's *Traité du vide* at hand, in particular the section dealing with the quarrel of the ancients and moderns. Pascal suggested that "the whole series of men, during the course of all the centuries, should be considered as a single man who lives forever and who is learning continually (Br.p.79-80)." He is merely concerned with a distinction, like that recently offered by Crane Brinton in the introduction to his *Ideas and Men* between cumulative and non-cumulative knowledge. For Pascal, scientific knowledge could be carried forward while religious knowledge could only grasp and preserve the given Truth. In the eyes of Ballanche, however, Pascal has found the formula by which God has united the generations of man: "When Pascal said that man knows only what has been taught him, and that consequently we cannot avoid returning to a primitive source, as to a first cause, he began to erect the bridge which would one day unite the ancient world and the new world." It is quite true that Pascal considered mankind united under the theological doctrine of original sin and that he understood the implications for the future of experimental science. But it is unlikely that he would have joined very enthusiastically in the somewhat mystical conclusion of Ballanche: "That the human species, in its ensemble, forms a sort of single whole, which would put us on the way to furnishing additional proof of the doctrine of solidarity."

In perfect innocence Ballanche wanders far from the intentions o his guide. His thought in the *Palingénésie sociale* is synthetic, th expression poetic; Pascal's is analytical, the expression dramatic an logical. Pascal saw an infinite gulf between the physical and th moral worlds, so wide that only human faith and will combined wit divine grace could bridge them. For Ballanche they are no longe distinct areas of experience, but an "identity: it is the primitive forn of the human mind." That is, moral and physical laws combine t form the structure of mind. Man does not have to conquer th meaning of his life from an alien world, as Pascal suggested; it i given to him by the elements of his universe. So for Pascal the abso lute and inescapable fact of the existence of man, the exile, was th inherence of evil, the awful suspension between being and nothing ness. Ballanche on the contrary finds the universe a proper settin; for man: it is a City of Expiation designed for the salvation of al men by a benevolent God. He has thus transformed a Platonic no tion of metempsychosis into *palingénésie*, the salvation of all mei by rebirth into a purifying society.[9] By the addition of this functior society becomes a religious instrument and the good is considerec "necessary and absolute," evil "conditional and contingent." Th gentle Ballanche is so convinced of the essential goodness of God tha he considers sin neutralized by the Redemption and condemns the notion of eternal damnation as a falsification of the new law o: Christianity.[10]

Ballanche is a spokesman for the new humanism of the nine teenth century. He sees the significance of individual lives in the un folding of human history. Only in the broad outlines of his doctrin and the personal commitment to Christianity do we see the imprin of Pascal. Ballanche continues to interpret the present condition o society as the result of Christian truths and traditions. With Pasca he presents man as a Good-seeker: "The spirit of man is always ir quest of the nourishment which he needs." Yet the thirst of Pascaliar man is never satisfied, while Ballanche concludes, "and he will alway: find it." Ballanche has adapted Pascal to the spirit of the times. H has brought a wealth of Pascalian themes into the literature of the period where they will interweave with the writings of Chateaubriand and Lamartine. He has also introduced a modified version of Pascal to the social optimists and thus to Auguste Comte "who at that date belonged to the Saint-Simonist family and who certainly profited from it."[11] This is how the new man of the nineteenth century sought to fuse the ethical insight of the seventeenth century with the political aspirations of the eighteenth.

FRANCOIS-RENE DE CHATEAUBRIAND (1768-1848). The three traditionalists of whom we have spoken felt that the evils of the Revolution were caused by the tragic flaw of eighteenth-century philosophy: the pridefulness of human wisdom. The themes which appear most vital to them are therefore expiation, conversion and re-dedication. If Joseph de Maistre examines intuitive techniques, it is not so much to increase his understanding of man as to find new forms of faith. In his religious as well as in his social thought, Lamennais is looking for a moral purpose in which he could submerge his stormy ego. Men such as these, together with the official leaders of the church, provide the core of formal religious thought during the Romantic period.

For the Romantic poet, however, Christianity speaks with no such voice of authority. In the works of Vigny, Lamartine, Musset and Hugo, religion, nature and human relationships acquire form and life only as they are distilled through the emotions of the sensitive individual. Religion does not come to these poets as imperatives to action. It echoes from the church bells heard in childhood, it mingles with the memories of human love and sometimes burns with the incandescence of personal suffering and disillusionment. In the eyes of the Romantic, religion was a passion, and not always a useful one. This attitude appears soon after the Revolution among the Neo-Christians: Ballanche, Chênedollé, Fontanes, Joubert and Chateaubriand. It has been condemned by more intransigent critics as being weak, vacillating and adolescent, and the Romantic has been defined as one who: "wears his hair long, garbs himself in outlandish costumes, cultivates eccentricity, and endeavors to make every act of his life one of open defiance to established social convention."[12] With Chateaubriand, however, we shall observe the combination of religious feeling and emotional awareness which adds dignity and universality to the apparently self-centered Romantic artist.

71

Like Lamennais, François de Chateaubriand was a Breton, a restless spirit and a wanderer. Unlike his zealous compatriot, however, Chateaubriand was less interested in building convictions than in tasting the many-flavored fruits of the world. His trip to America in 1791 filled his senses with odors, sounds and scenes which furnish the exotic background for many of his subsequent writings. While Lamennais needed friends and disciples, Chateaubriand needed the love of women. During his final illness, he required the constant presence of Mme Récamier, certainly not because of the ministrations which she could provide, as she was nearly an invalid herself, but because in her company alone it was possible for him to establish that continuity of feeling which for him meant life itself. There is a strong element of melodrama in Chateaubriand's habit of attaching absolute value to each distinct moment of feeling, but there is also continuity of esthetic, religious and intellectual feeling. René may find himself tossed from one emotional peak to the next, but in the *Génie du christianisme*, *Etudes historiques* and *Vie de Rancé*, he discovers an esthetic stimulus in Christianity which changes the tastes of a generation, a new interpretation of Christian history and an unwavering devotion to the religion which inspired him.

THE ROMANTIC PSYCHE AND REVOLT. With his natural sensuality, Chateaubriand would have seemed better fitted to defend the spontaneous passions of the "noble savage" than the spirit of Christianity. But there is another factor in the composition of his personality which establishes that state of soul characteristic of the Romantic. It is the phychic process of deferred action. Between the pure, original emotion and the activity which it should produce, there appears a hesitation, an almost fatal suspension of effort. To the observer, this indecision of the will constitutes a baffling inconsistency on the part of the subject who, in turn, experiences life as a series of unfulfilled promises. Chateaubriand approached America partly as an explorer in search of the mythical northwest passage. His discoveries were all intangible, however: scenes and sounds and a profound sense of solitude. His marriage must have represented some unformulated desire to attach himself to a normal, fundamental human experience. It was not successful. An exterior obstacle intervened: the Revolution and exile. This experience apparently fixed in him the attitude of "deferment" so that he appears to have forgotten the very existence of his mate until a serious romance with Charlotte Ives had flourished at Bungay, England: another instance of conflicting purposes and inner contradictions.

Chateaubriand is by no means at the mercy of this turmoil. He is acutely aware of his lack of unity and direction. René confesses to Chactas and Father Souel: "I am accused of having inconsistent tastes, of not being able to enjoy the same chimera for very long, of being prey to an imagination which plunges to the depths of my pleasures, as if it were afraid of their endurance; they accuse me of always striving beyond the goal which I am able to reach: alas! I am merely pursuing an unknown good toward which I am instinctively drawn. Is it my fault if I find limitations everywhere, if finite things have no value for me?" In this troubled mind we would scarcely expect to find the seeds of a distinguished statesman and Christian apologist. Yet in the early nineteenth-century we find Chateaubriand undertaking a remarkably "engaged" position in the life of society. We shall examine the effect of solitude and lonely meditation on a passionate but uncommitted nature in the *Essai sur les révolutions* and the subsequent integration offered by the *Génie du Christianisme*, in which the influence of Pascal produces such striking effects.

The main body of the *Essai sur les Révolutions* presents a comparative study of the revolutionary movements in ancient Greece and in modern Europe. The purpose of this comparison is supposedly to shed light on contemporary events in France and to permit a certain amount of prophesying as to the course these events would take in the following century. The result is a series of unconvincing parallels, in which the Jacobin party is compared to the military state of Sparta, for example, and a hopeless future is forecast for the states of Europe. What is most noticeably lacking to the work is a controlling idea which would give some meaning to the apparently senseless rise and decline of civilizations. Nowhere does the author find a single ray of hope to modify his bleak conclusion that "The history of mankind is a ladder of misery and revolutions are its different rungs." It is essential to recognize the origin of the *Génie* in the unconscious despair of the *Essai*.

The religious thought of the *Essai* is even more bitter. Chateaubriand occasionally recognizes the hand of God in the untouched splendor of nature: "There is a God. The grasses of the valley and the cedars of Lebanon bless Him. . . . man alone has said: There is no God." At the moment the author is a most unhappy man. Here is a summary of his chapter on the "Objections of the *philosophes* against Christianity": God made man in the knowledge that man would sin, and then punished him for sinning; such a cruel Creator is unworthy of our adoration. The Christian dogma and discipline were derived from pagan sources, and we must conclude that there is no true religion on earth. There is no proof of the literal accuracy or even the authenticity of the New Testament. From the invasion of Rome to the Renaissance, the Church has fed upon ignorance and has marched like a giant towards despotism. The venality of the Catholic clergy is as great as that of the ancient Greek divine, but the tight-knit organization of the Catholic Church permits more exploitation than anything available to the isolated Greek guardians of shrines. Auricular confession teaches innocent children to use the language of vice before they could have any knowledge of it. Throughout the *Essai* the phrase, "The fall of Christianity," resounds with the same finality as Gibbon's famous description of the fate of the Roman Empire.

If, as Paula Hey suggests, the continuity between the *Essai* and the *Génie du christianisme* is based on a Pascalian sense of the "misery and greatness" of man, we must admit that little of man's potential greatness can be found in the earlier work.[13] It is painfully clear that the *Essai* is the product of the passionate side of Chateaubriand's nature, without the balance and control of his later works. In 1826 he returns to the writing which has been pounced upon by critics as evidence of hypocrisy on the part of the author of the *Génie*. He attempts to correct and modify the more nihilistic passages of the *Essai* in detailed footnotes, but there are moments when the pen falls from the author's nerveless fingers as he recognizes the exposed, tormented specter of the "evil genius" which continues to threaten him, but which is now his servant rather than his master. The *Génie du christianisme* is simply the other face of the coin. Within the space of a few years Chateaubriand has brought stability out of confusion, love out of anger and hope out of despair.

THE *GENIE* AND PASCAL. Chateaubriand's long descriptions of bizarre forms in nature, his "poetics" and his preoccupation with the outward effects of cult, monuments and ruins have led nineteenth-century critics to deny him full stature as a Christian thinker. The Catholic author, Louis Veuillot, suggests that while he may have possessed Christian feelings, "he did not understand the meaning of Christianity." Sainte-Beuve's classic portrait shows an "Epicurean with a Catholic imagination." Certainly Chateaubriand lacks Pascal's singleness of purpose. Where the other-worldliness of Christianity assumes an exclusive position in the life of Pascal, for Chateaubriand it merges with the esthetic experience, controlling and dignifying it. This explains why tears play the same role in the *Génie* as does anxiety in the *Pensées*. When Chateaubriand speaks about the "reality of tears," he is saying that the God of Christianity is a healing agency for man's emotional wounds, while Pascal conceives Him as the resolution of psychic anguish for a humanity which had lost its personal sense of the Good in the fall from grace. Chateaubriand is one of the very few friends to stand by Lamennais after his imprisonment and rejection by the church. He is even in sympathy with Lamennais' social doctrines, but when he is urged to condemn the Christian faith on the basis of the arbitrary and autocratic decisions from Rome, he will only reply: "I wish to believe." This firmness on the part of Chateaubriand does not indicate the fury of conviction sometimes bred from fear or hopelessness, but rather the recognition of an acquired truth by which he had succeeded in transforming the confused world of his adolescence into the sufficiently comprehensible universe of maturity.

There can be no doubt that Pascal played a large part in the conception of the *Génie du christianisme*. In a final paragraph, Chateaubriand gives the following quotation from the *Pensées* to indicate the structure of his own work: "For those who find religion repugnant, we must begin by showing them that it is not contrary to reason; then that it is venerable and merits respect; we must make it desirable and encourage the hope that it is true; and after that show by incontestable proof that it is true; demonstrate its greatness and worth by its longevity and holiness." Of his section devoted to philosophy (Part III, Book II), no chapter is more deeply moving than that devoted to Pascal. It is here that the "Romantic Pascal" was created, the portrait of a precocious genius, detached from the world by his knowledge of sorrow and by a "mysterious feeling of immensity." This is the Pascal whose Pensées are transmitted to us as shadows, incomplete, "the ruins of Palmyra."[14] But beside this "ineffective," historical figure, Chateaubriand recognizes another, more living personality, the one whom Voltaire had called a "sublime madman." Here is the man of flesh, acquainted with human weaknesses and a more terrible foe of social injustice and political inequality than Rousseau. When he considers the enflamed sensitivity of Pascal, combined with his extraordinary powers of perception, Chateaubriand trembles to think "what this great man would have become if he had not been Christian!" As a critic, Chateaubriand has reached a level of identification where what he says of Pascal holds a double meaning for himself. We shall see this process repeated in the *Vie de Rancé*.

What sort of a document is the *Génie du christianisme*? The book undoubtedly made a greater impact on the religious thought of the early Romantic period than did the *Pensées*, and yet it cannot be considered a finished piece of apologetic literature. The answer to the riddle turns upon the way in which Chateaubriand understood Christianity. In the first place there is a demonstration of the truths of Christianity, of uneven degrees of sincerity: the first Book immerses the reader in every form of apology including the utilitarian, the symbolic validity of the Trinity (especially popular with Joseph de Maistre and the mystics of Lyons at this time), a descriptive and lyrical tribute to cult, and even an appeal to the authority of the Church Fathers (a method which he had decried in his opening chapter). But there is also the omnipresent figure of René. Deprived of his normal social development by the Revolution, Chateaubriand, like Wordsworth, is driven to cultivate the world of self. Thus his recollections of childhood, the first movements of his heart and the magic response to nature fuse into a single religious insight. This explains the free, vagabond way in which Chateaubriand explores many inviting paths of experience, with assurance that religious meaning will be discovered in the process. His treatment of the concept of original sin gives an excellent example of a poetic imagination which takes unfettered flight from traditional positions, unconscious of its novelty.

Chateaubriand's approach to the question of original sin is perfectly similar to Pascal's statement of the double revelation in human consciousness of depravity and divinity. The author of the *Génie* asks: "How, without that early stain, can we account for the vicious tendency of our nature, opposed by a voice which tells us that we were formed for virtue?" (*Génie* I, 1, 4). Like Pascal, Chateaubriand describes the misery of human life, the injustice and the need for a religious principle which would redeem this apparently senseless creation. As for the inner conflict which is the essence of morality, Chateaubriand resumes Pascal's narrative of the dual principles of the embattled self: "A perpetual clash exists between his understanding and his desire, between his reason and his heart." Were he similar to the rest of creation, as are other animals, man's reason would be synchronized with his passions, but his experience of inner oppositions indicates that he is distinct from the rest of creation and that he has evolved from a preceding, superior unity. Change, division and inner warfare are, for Pascal and Chateaubriand, both the manifestation and the logical proof of original sin: "For, by the chain of logic and the probabilities of analogy, original sin is rediscovered, since man, as we know him, is not at all like earliest man" (*Génie*, I, 3,3).[15]

After the descriptive statement of the condition of man and the traditional resolution of original sin, Chateaubriand leaves Pascal to pass by way of Rousseau to a formula of his own. A first sign of this departure appears in Chateaubriand's portrait of Adam. Had he been willing to follow Pascal through this course of reasoning, he would have turned to a biblical, theological vision of an almost angelic figure whose transformation into nearly animal form is an incomprehensible mystery for which Christianity alone possesses the key: "These are things which took place in a state of nature completely different from ours, and which exceed the state of our present capacity" (Br. p.583). On the contrary, Chateaubriand conceives of an Adam similar to Rousseau's *primitive man*, "the most enlightened and the best of men." Like Rousseau, Chateaubriand finds it nearly impossible to distinguish between love and feeling. This love, or life of the senses, enters into no moral equation; it is rather a fragment of the created universe, like air or water. On this basis Chateaubriand concludes that Adam could not have sinned by excess of love or passion: "this would have been worthy of pity rather than punishment." The sin of Adam is rather that of the eighteenth-century rationalist, the sin of intellectual curiosity. In fact, the primary role of Christianity is to combat the philosophic impulse in man: "and if Adam had become guilty by having wished to *experience* too much, rather than to *conceive* too much, man could perhaps have redeemed himself and the Son of the Eternal might not have been obliged to immolate himself" (*Génie* I, 3,3). Fortunately, Chateaubriand does not follow this apology for the gentle passion to its logical conclusion, or he would have established a new cult in which *agape* would have become much more like *eros*. Once again the emotional spontaneity which might plunge Chateaubriand into successive abysses of frustration is checked by the religion to which he has confided the guidance of his heart.

This leads us to a necessary comparison of the connotations which the "heart" holds for Pascal and for Chateaubriand. Here lies the full range of distinction between the ascetic Christian savant and the melodious Christian troubadour. The breadth of Pascal's conception may be found in the three categories into which his study of the "heart" is divided. On the sensate level of animal passions, it may be the unguided principle of concupiscence: "How empty and full of filth is the heart of man!" On the rational level, it is the source of intuitive knowledge as opposed to demonstrable logic: it is the instrument by which we are permitted to assume that there are three dimensions in space and that number is infinite, while reason operates within this "given" sphere: "principles are felt, propositions are deduced; and the whole result is certitude, reached by different routes" (Stewart 630-Br.282). Finally, the heart is the giver of religious knowledge: "Tis the heart, not reason that feels God" (Stewart 627-Br. 277). Corresponding to the three orders of things: flesh, reason and will, the heart does not oppose reason, but as the intuitive element of ethical and intellectual knowledge, it identifies the religious nature of man which is beyond the scope of analysis.

Countless critics have suggested that the *Génie* is no more than a prolonged expression of Pascal's conception of the heart.[16] At times Chateaubriand does appear to hover on the brink of Pascalian insight. He reaffirms that Christianity has "shown the heights and depths of our heart, which is full of contrasts, as are we." But for Chateaubriand, this is not the organ which grasps the mystery of life and demands the touch of God; it remains the organ of human affections. Even the religion which explains the heart smiles upon the emotions: "Christianity, we say, seen in the light of these contrasts (of the heart) is yet, par excellence, the religion of friendship" (*Génie*, II, 3, 1). This Christianity of Chateaubriand which enhances the emotional life also indicates the alien nature of the intellect, and "if it is concerned with the nature of intellectual being, it is also concerned with our own being" (*Génie*, II, 2, 1). Pascal sees man defined by intellect, a "thinking reed." Chateaubriand defines man by his feeling and sensitivity. Even in his most ethical thought, in a later chapter on vice and virtue, Chateaubriand gives an esthetic turn to the problem, showing the gulf between the seventeenth-century moralist and the romantic genius:

> We must not always take soundings in the abysses of the heart: the truths that it contains are of the sort which require half-light and perspective. It is unwise to apply reason too often to the part of our being which loves, to bring a rational mind to bear upon the passions (*Génie*, II 3,1).

This, then is the key to Chateaubriand's apology: the utilization of the Christian explanation of moral concepts, with particular attention to Pascal's interpretation of man as the battleground between physical and spiritual natures; the transformation of this concept into its poetic or intuitive content; and finally, the descriptive investigation of this content as opposed to that of the pagan concept, so that the validity of Christianity is demonstrated by its inevitably greater proximity to the original intuiton. The proofs do not compel assent or rejection, as do Pascal's. But the positive contribution which Chateaubriand has made to Christian apologetics is to demonstrate with power and conviction the contribution of Christianity to the esthetic and cultural development of modern civilization.

With a religion of esthetic dimensions, it is not surprising that Chateaubriand discovers a humanity which is neither the rationally fashioned creature of deism nor the redeemable sinner of traditional, ascetic Christianity. According to his new doctrine, God created absolute duration in time and progressive duration in space, moved by esthetic considerations of unity and variety: "without the first there would have been no greatness in the creation, and without the other there would have been monotony" (*Génie*, 1,5,2). The creation was therefore designed for some spectator other than God, for whom the relative concepts of greatness and monotony could have no significance. From his own visual sensitivity, Chateaubriand infers that man's role on earth is that of *spectator*. From *René* to the *Life of Rancé* there flows a constant stream of images experienced as bits of creation, then reintegrated with their divine origins. The condition of the atheist is made untenable by his most natural gestures: "Has he never, then, in his misfortunes, raised his eyes towards heaven, or in his happiness, lowered his glance towards earth?" (*Génie*, 1,5,2). It would be absurd to question the purity of the religious convictions of Christianity's staunchest defender, both before the Concordat and after the failure of the Restoration. Yet it is clear that Chateaubriand's Christianity seldom passes beyond the rich variety of the physical universe, and that the object of the religious experience is not so much union with the absolute as the establishment of some harmonious emotional balance, where inspiration leads not to intensity but to a sustained feeling of transcendence.

AN INTERPRETATION OF HISTORY. The problems which Chateaubriand deals with in the *Etudes historiques* are those which have proved crucial to the survival of Christian faith in post-Revolutionary Europe. Can Christianity occupy any significant position in a world awake to the potentiality of reason and science? Does religion possess the social and philosophical dimensions needed by a swiftly-changing society? Can Saint Augustine's City of God, raised once from the ruins of Europe, arise again on the soil of a continent stained with the blood of thousands seeking justice and freedom in the immediate world of the present? The traditionalist philosophers were speaking affirmatively. But to the extent that they failed to accept the depth of revolutionary sentiment or the impossibility of reviving the institutions of the past unchanged, Bonald, Maistre and Lamennais were unequal to the task. The more flexible historical relativism of Chateaubriand offers a promising method of reconciling modern man with his historical institutions and yet not imprisoning him within the walls of a predetermined social orthodoxy.

It is important to understand the evolution in historical perspective between the generation of Pascal and that of Chateaubriand. Both Pascal and Bossuet spoke to minds formed by the classical spirit. The body-soul dichotomy was generally accepted and there was no difficulty conceiving a given "spiritual" context in which the relative histories of human societies might run their course. Thus, human history mirrored the immutable purpose of God. And so Bossuet could reasonably interpret the universal history of man as a Christian event. For the Christian historian secular societies rise and fall according to their spiritual accomplishments or failures; true history, however, is written in the fall, the redemption, the founding of the church and the final consummation. The problem of the historian, then, is to arrange the specific events of human societies into a pattern with these fixed landmarks. For Pascal this meant that history itself was a miraculous demonstration of divine intention, and Christianity was fully justified through its miracles. But from Hume's "Essay on Miracles" to Voltaire's "Pucelle," no concept was more brutally demolished than the claims of any society to such privileged dispensations of God's grace. Modern history is written from an inductive basis, like that of Voltaire and Hume, in which patterns are sought to unify the available data, or from a philosophical premise like that of Vico or Hegel in which a universal dynamics such as "intellection" or "synthesis" is used to explain the past and predict the future. Chateaubriand is one of the first historians to adopt a relativist interpretation of Christianity for the purpose of showing its vitality:

Nothing is forced to accommodate itself in my system, or rather in the corrected system of Bossuet; it is the system which is made to accommodate the facts and which contains society while leaving

81

it the freedom of action. . . . Christianity is not a fixed circle, it is on the contrary a circle which widens as civilization grows, it does not limit, it attacks no science, no liberty (*Etudes historiques*, IV,I, p.139).

The element which Chateaubriand adds to seventeenth-century apology is that of social realism. This is one of the important keys to the mind of Chateaubriand: a faith which provides the necessary context for judgment, and an intellect attuned to the ideal yet imaginatively aware of human relativity.

Unlike the traditionalists, Chateaubriand does not condemn the writers of the *Encyclopedia* for the horrors of the Revolution. The truths which the *philosophes* brought to light must be recognized and their errors revised. For Chateaubriand, one of the most striking errors of the preceding century was the unsuccessful attempt to define human history in terms of an abstract and distant divine reason, incapable of inspiring the modern world. By dismissing historical Christianity as an accidental, external social phenomenon, the rationalists had overlooked the deep roots of Christian ethics in the hearts of the majority in France even during the Revolution. Chateaubriand correctly points out that "the book of modern history will remain closed to you if you do not consider Christianity either as a revelation which has brought about a social transformation or as a natural progression of the human mind towards the great civilization" (*Etudes historiques*, IV, I, p.144). Both of these interpretations suggest rich material for philosophic speculation, and Chateaubriand makes his contribution to the philosophy of history by investigating each.

The meaning given by Chateaubriand to revelation is undoubtedly derived from that of Pascal. For the latter the divine plan is inscribed in human nature in two ways: intellectually, by man's dependence on intuition for knowledge of first principles, and morally, by the discrepancy between man's absolute goals and finite means of attaining them. The philosophical and ethical criteria for religious truth are found by Chateaubriand, as by Pascal, to lie in the fact that: "Christianity is composed of the highest and most abstract philosophy concerning the nature of God and of the most perfect ethics relative to the nature of man . . ." (*Etudes historiques*, IV, I, pp.146-147).

82

For both thinkers, Christianity represents the intention of God immediately present to the deepest sources of human thought and action. But here an important distinction must be made. Behavior and intellection are modes of present time, and while these play an active part in the Pascalian cosmos, they are conditioned with reference to a doctrinally defined past. Man's future for the orthodox Christian has frequently been either an inscrutable "beyond" or the perpetual resuscitation of an all-important past, unchanged and unchangeable since the appearance in the world of Christ. Chateaubriand, like Lamennais, recognizes the legitimate aspirations of society, perhaps not to Utopia, but at least to a continuity in which the sacrifices and ideals of the present might improve slightly upon the failures of the past to produce a better society.

From this point of view we can understand the insistence on the prophecies and miracles in the *Pensées* and on the history of the early church in the *Etudes historiques*. Pascal's objective is the attainment of "charity," a supernatural experience depending on the action of Christ upon the heart of man; Chateaubriand, in the *Etudes*, has moved to a conception of social perfectibility guided but not contained by Christian doctrine. The originality of Chateaubriand is his conversion of Christian doctrine into an optimistic, utilitarian philosophy of society: "Christianity grows and moves with time; enlightenment when it associates with the mental faculties, feeling when it associates with the movements of the soul; moderator of peoples and kings, it combats only the excess of power, from whatever direction it comes ... it is the act of perfecting society" (*Etudes historiques*, IV, I, pp. 149-152). The author will frequently point out that the Christianity to which he refers is "true cult," and the doctrine embraced is essentially that of Roman Catholicism, so purely conceived that it does not even suggest the question of gallicanism or ultramontanism. But the context is of the nineteenth century; with deliberation it applies the ancient doctrine to the contemporary question of man's capacity for political fulfillment.

RANCÉ, PORT-ROYAL REVISITED. The vicissitudes of public life touch the final years of Chateaubriand's life with heavy strains of pessimism, deepened by the impossibility of the youthful, passionate nature of René to make a compromise with the humiliating demands of old age. The *Vie de Rancé* offers an unexpected panorama of the type of faith with which Chateaubriand approached his death. The work was undertaken as a spiritual exercise at the advice of his counselor, the abbé Séguin. Chateaubriand confesses that the task was for some time repugnant to him, but before long the affinities between the experiences of the seventeenth-century reformer and his own permit him to analyse in Rancé those values dearest to himself. In the course of this study, Chateaubriand examines the texture of Rancé's total, self-obliterating faith, seen in the perspective of his own poetic vision. His goal becomes the nearly impossible one of vocalizing the self-annihilating silence of the Trappist.

In a sense Chateaubriand's study of Rancé represents a return to his earlier relationship with Pascal. Through the eyes of Rancé he is able to give a more intimate picture of Port-Royal to his generation than could Sainte-Beuve. But the distance between the two spokesmen for Christianity is clearly visible. Pascal is now seen "haunted by doubt," seeking salvation by flinging himself on faith. There is the same awesome mystery in this tortured faith as in that which surrounds the Christian monasticism of Rancé: "What would be horrible, if it were not admirable, is the unsurmountable barrier which he has placed between himself and his readers. Never a confession, never does he speak of what he has done, of his errors and repentance" (*Vie de Rancé*, p.244). Through Pascal Chateaubriand discovered the philosophical significance of Christianity; in Rancé he studies the Christian meaning of death. But the Christianity which is characteristic of Chateaubriand is of the essence of life in the world of sensual forms. For this reason he says of Rancé: "This life does not satisfy, it lacks a springtime." On the other hand there is in the life of Chateaubriand a springtime which never completely fades. The rich emotions with which his life is studded are like so many bouquets which he may, with voluptuousness, yet with respect, lay at the altar of his faith.

This transformation of religious meaning into personal visions was destined to be more fruitful poetically than philosphically. By refusing the core of doctrine and belief, Baudelaire and Rimbaud evoke moral rather than religious intuitions. The confessional motivation of the symbolist is reminiscent of Chateaubriand, but pessimism and passion have lost the gentle warmth which Christianity added to the spiritual Odyssey of René. The vague, nostalgic melancholy with which Chateaubriand established the rights of religious feeling seems to have expressed those unique emotions which make up the romantic complex. They did not prove transmissable to a machine-age society. The great contribution of Chateaubriand seems to have been his application of religious lyricism to the problems of the modern mind. He understood and impressed Pascal on the imagination of his century; he encouraged the growth of religious sensitivity in post-Revolutionary Europe. Through the evolution of his own moral and intellectual life he showed his generation how to be faithful to a tradition and yet as free as an anarchist, how to champion religion without losing a note of personal feeling. No voice spoke more authoritatively or appealingly for a religion and a government of free, creative minds.

Academicians and Moralists

ANTOINE DE RIVAROL (1753-1801). The introduction of Pascal into the concerns of nineteenth-century philosophy came from an unsuspected source: the worldly and witty Antoine de Rivarol.[1] From his *Discours sur l'universalité de la langue française* (1784) to the *Discours préliminaire du nouveau dictionnaire de la langue française* (1797), Rivarol evolves from rationalist systems of thought to the philosophy of experience which is central to the investigations of Biran and Bergson.

In two *Lettres à M. Necker* (1788), Rivarol attacks the bourgeois utilitarian ethics which seemed to coincide with the rationalism and materialism of the century. Necker had just published his *Importance des idées religieuses*, in which he called for the application of religion to society as a sedative for the mounting tensions of the Revolution. Rivarol points out that morality is not a patent medicine to be ladled out as needed, but a "ray which enlightens all men coming into the world. . . . It is in this way that God has revealed himself to men" (*Deuxième lettre*, pp.31-32). The notion that man was made for religious response, that religion was not a by-product of society, indicates the new direction of metaphysical, moral and religious thought in France at the turn of the century.

In his *Discours préliminaire* and a *Récapitulation* written shortly before his death, Rivarol introduces a characteristic of reality which suggests much of the future course of philosophy in France. The concept of "innate needs" is designed to counteract the rationalism of Descartes' "innate ideas." It advances a personalistic attitude toward life in the satisfaction of given needs. It provides pragmatic justification both for rational philosophy which satisfies the need to speculate and for religion which satisfies the need to embrace truth with love and hope. On this broad base, Rivarol introduces the "heart" of Pascal as an instrument of intuitive knowledge. It is no longer society, but the self, which constitutes the focal point of investigation. Rivarol revives a Cartesian movement of ideas, an inward vision, but this inner universe is found to be the one which Pascal described in his *Pensées*.

PIERRE LAROMIGUIÈRE (1756-1837). Two of the academic philosophers most responsible for the revival of philosophic studies and the direction which they took after the ravages of Napoleon, were Laromiguière and Royer-Collard. Both developed out of religious backgrounds. Laromiguière had been ordained as a priest, although during the Revolution he dropped his clerical status. Royer-Collard had been raised in the pure Jansenist atmosphere of Sompuis which had preserved the austerity of Port-Royal since the dispersal of 1709-1711.[2] Both became exponents of secular philosophical systems by which they sought to strike a balance between the extremes of eighteenth-century materialism and the religious reaction under Napoleon. Both were faced with the fact that Condillac's sensationalism was still the most compelling doctrine in French philosophy. Laromiguière, as a disciple of Condillac, attempted to modify the master's system, perhaps beyond the bounds of rigorous logic, to include the existence of the soul and the notion of immortality. Royer-Collard discovered the sympathetic doctrine of common-sense of the Scottish philosopher, Thomas Reid, whose Presbyterian morality, combining as it did the practical with the spiritual, was not foreign to Royer-Collard's Jansenism. The movement of thought initiated by these two men accounted directly for the success of Cousin's more politically-inspired eclecticism and lead indirectly but surely to the later formation of Bergsonian intuitive philosophy and William James' pragmatism.

THE NEW DUALISM. Laromiguière is known chiefly through the *Leçons de Philosophie*, 1815-1818, taken from his course at the Faculté des Lettres and revised, though not seriously altered, as his continuing popularity created a need for new editions. The method and the starting point are those of Condillac: the observation of events in nature, the logical organization of these events and their relation to an emergent principle. Like Condillac, Laromiguière is primarily concerned with the origin of ideas, but for him the distinction between ideas produced by the senses and ideas as pure experience in themselves suggest the need for more than a single originating principle. So the *Leçons* posit two states of being: one in which man is the passive recipient of external impulsions, and another in which he becomes actively attentive to the outer world. The resulting dualism was so contrary to the philosophy of Condillac that by 1858 Laromiguière was identified as "one of the first who reacted against the desolating doctrines of Locke and Condillac, Cabanis and de Tracy,"[3] a judgment which would have profoundly shocked or amused him. In the formulation of his idea of the intuitive basis for our knowledge of first principles and his description of the spiritual side of human nature, Laromiguière owes much to Pascal and it is from this point of view that we shall evaluate the contribution of the *Leçons* to the course of French philosophy.

The logic of Laromiguière is reminiscent of the analytical procedure of Condillac: it assumes that when an event has been defined, its identity has thereby been established. Pascal, on the contrary, points out that a definition merely presents a new event which must also be defined. For this reason, in the *Réflexions sur la géométrie en générale,* he concludes that we "are in a natural and immutable helplessness to treat any science whatever in an absolutely complete order." Against this apparently discouraging judgment of human science, Laromiguière protests that "we will have a complete order every time that, in the exposition of a science, the basic words have been determined by perception, by experience, and all the others by these first words" (*Leçons,* I, p.395); that is to say, whenever an undefinable term has been reached. The distinction between the two is largely one of metaphysical tension. For Pascal, the significance of the fact that no science is final is that for finality man must turn to God, and that other means than those of science must be found for investigating ultimate truth. Laromiguière recognizes the suprarational nature of first principles, but is unwilling to sacrifice the claims of science to those of supernaturalism.

Unwilling to grasp at any arbitrary synthesis, Laromiguière presents mind and matter as primary elements which philosophy must attempt to define in terms suitable to their own type of reality. On the paradoxical fusion of these two elements in man, Laromiguière gives his complete adherence to Pascal's definition: "Man is to himself the most prodigious object in nature; (for) he cannot conceive what a body is and even less how a body can be united to a mind, and yet that is his own being." This acceptance of a spiritual mode of knowing does not mean the rejection of sensational philosophy and science. Larmiguière's combination of the two schools of thought is found in varying degrees in the works of Destutt de Tracy, Cabanis and Biran. He is attempting to correct the limitations of materialistic monism and to reopen the question of the soul and the mystery of life.

It is evidently less to unity of the system than to the integrity and humility of their author that the *Leçons* owed their popularity. He is one of the first of the academic philosophers to identify the role of Pascal as a champion of the dignity of human reason. Citing the *pensée* "Should the universe crush him, man would yet be more noble than that which kills him, because he knows that he is dying . . . ,". Laromiguière continues with several pages of vigorous exposition, concluding: "It is therefore because he thinks, that he knows and that he knows himself, that man holds the first rank. By his form he was undoubtedly one of the most admirable works of the Divinity. By his intelligence he has become the image" (*Leçons*, II, pp.26-27). Thus an alliance is formed in the mind of Laromiguière between scientific method and religious truth, and there is a clarity and precision of statement which make the union harmonious. Unlike the eclecticism which replaces it, this philosophy does not embrace any and all criteria of truth. It remains rather within the French tradition of speculative thought, relating perceptive observations of human psychology to their proper metaphysical context. In this work the spirit of Pascal moves surely and potently. It has unquestionably set its mark on Laromiguière, whose remarks near the conclusion of the *Leçons* almost paraphrase the *Pensées*: "Above all do not forget that the supreme intelligence, embracing all, simultaneously, needs neither our general ideas nor our reason; and that all the sciences which the genius of man has created at so great a cost are only a *magnificent testimonial* to his weakness" (*Leçons*, II, p.415).

By pressing more deeply into sensationalist epistemology, Laromiguière discovered the need for a dynamic system quite distinct from the mechanical operations of sense data. Without falling into Pascal's scepticism, he nevertheless found in the writings of Pascal the inevitability of limits at the beginning and end of all rational sequences. From Pascal he also learned the implications of the unknowable in describing the relationship of man to God. The multiplicity of interests of the eclectics will tend to diminish this preoccupation with Pascal, although Victor Cousin devoted much time and energy to the restoration of the *Pensées* to their proper form. However, the decisive impact of his thought on the newly forming schools of nineteenth-century philosophy is a fact which history continues to clarify.

PIERRE-PAUL ROYER-COLLARD (1763-1843). Royer-Collard's philosophy contains two parts: one in which he criticizes ideology and one in which he proposes a "philosophy of perception." The critique of Condillac is based on applying the doctrine of sensationalism to all the legitimate questions of philosophy, pointing out the weakness of the doctrine in all but a few areas. What explanation, asks Royer-Collard, can the ideologist give of the notions of substance, cause, space and time? If these general or abstract notions are facts for which philosophy must give some account, then a doctrine which limits knowledge to the testimony of the senses must be condemned as inadequate. For what sense can produce the idea of identity or eternity? Touch, sight, sound, smell and hearing could never arrive by their own evidence or by their collaboration at the notion of a universal reality. If the senses are the unique originators of ideas, the entire category of general ideas becomes a monstrous illusion.

Against the scepticism of Hume and the sense-centered philosophy of Locke and Condillac, Royer-Collard points to a consciousness and an activity which precede any meaningful sequence of sense experiences. In the new philosophy of perception, the primitive fact of understanding is therefore consciousness which reveals the self, followed by memory which assures continuity and duration, and volition from which the notion of causality arises. Royer-Collard is never quite definite as to whether the consciousness referred to is an intuitive faculty or an instinctive belief, but it is clear that his point of view is full of possibilities to be exploited later in the century by vitalists and supernaturalists alike.

George Boas suggests that Pascal was even more important in the formation of Royer-Collard's thought than in that of Laromiguière: "In contrast to Laromiguière, who had been illuminated by the brilliance of the eighteenth century, Royer-Collard received his light from the restrained glow of the seventeenth. He had no love of sceptics and sensationalists; he preferred the apologists. His reading was Pascal, Corneille, Bossuet, Milton—in English we are told."[4] It must not be assumed, however, that Royer-Collard offers no more than a reactionary, traditionalist philosophy. Like Pascal, he conceives reality in terms of eternity, but with the rationalists he sees human life as a functional part of the universe, the whole embraced by the same eternity: "Time loses itself in eternity, space in immensity. Without time there would be no duration; without space there would be no extension. Time and space contain in their ample breast all finite existences and they are contained in none." There is no incommensurable here, no antagonism between man and his setting. Pascal did not object to scepticism on the grounds that it sapped the basis of reason, but rather that it permitted the seeker to deny metaphysical truth as soon as reason faltered. Royer-Collard is more concerned with the need for intellectual order than with subjective states of the soul. His war with scepticism is directed against the threat to public morality: "As soon as it has penetrated the understanding, it invades it entirely."

The nineteenth-century Jansenist, like that of the seventeenth century, is committed to a moral doctrine with which he attempts to remold his generation. The new doctrine is one of balance, measure and logic. Royer-Collard proposes a new approach to the problems of philosophy, but continues to visualize these problems as the proper objective of human reason. There is no metaphysical anguish nor psychological tension in this moderate spiritualism. The psychology which Royer-Collard introduces is a legitimate study of the modes of being of a unique self, rather than that of an unidentifiable chain of sensations. It is typical of this groping period that the implications are never fully exploited and carried to their conclusions until after 1850 or even, in cases like that of Royer-Collard, until the appearance of Bergson.

JOSEPH-MARIE DEGERANDO (1772-1842). The two works of Degérando before the turn of the century, *De la génération des connaissances humaines,* and *Des signes et de l'art de penser,* clearly follow the lines of thought of Locke and Condillac. Knowledge is derived from sensation and thought is taken as the product of pressures from the outer world on the blank tablet of the mind. While Chateaubriand is bringing forth his *Génie du christianisme,* however, Degérando is preparing his *Histoire comparée des systèmes de philosophie relativement aux principes des connaissances humaines* (1803). In a sense the approach of Degérando constitutes a historical validation of the central thought of Condillac. Yet the author announces in his introduction that he would subject empirical as well as idealistic philosophical systems to critical analysis to show that "true systems should be founded on experience. . . (and) how they should develop from experience."[5] The experience to which Degérando refers extends beyond the life of the senses. So he reviews Descartes in the light of Condillac in order to identify the subjective and objective elements of cognition: "The first origin of knowledge is in exterior experience, its reality is based upon interior and exterior experience together; its certitude is guaranteed by interior experience alone" *(Hist. Comp.* III, p. 551). By reversing the Cartesian order of perception, Degérando tries to avoid the paradox of a phenomenal world known only as a mode of subjective thought. His synthesis is typical of the eclectic tendencies of the times.

A tradition of empirical prejudice against intellectual absolutism or idealism is evident in Degérando's treatment of classical and scholastic philosophy. Almost ignoring Plato, he has this to say of the period of Plotinus and the Alexandrian platonists: "For seven or eight centuries, philosophy has little more than shortcomings to be shown" *(Hist. comp.* I, p. 18). As for the Middle Ages, "The faults of the Scholastics are certainly too real to need exaggeration" *(Hist. comp.* III, p. 93). One of the few representatives of religious thought to win honorable mention is Pascal, and even here it is that side of

Pascal which deals with science which attracts attention. Referring to Pascal's distinction between first principles such as space, time and matter which are grasped intuitively, and propositions about them which must be demonstrated empirically, Degérando suggests that this is "the first example in which science is related entirely to the primitive and inexplicable sense of the truths of fact" (Hist. comp. III, pp. 49-50). The religious convictions of Pascal had been too closely identified with superstition to evoke serious analysis, but the respect of Degérando increases as he is led to review the degree to which the eighteenth century had failed to isolate and guarantee the rights of human reason.

THE PHILOSOPHY OF EXPERIENCE AND PASCAL. Degérando is the first to set forth a movement of ideas from Pascal and Tschirnhausen to Thomas Reid in which a rational instinct is found to be antecedent to the development and functioning of reason itself. In this new light, sensations would not be the images of external objects, "but their immediate perception" and the role of reason would be recognized as the processing of intuitively perceived truths (Hist. Comp., III, p. 93). The *philosophy of experience* cannot be used to defend any preconceived system of thought: it disapproves those who would "humiliate human reason to assure the success of beliefs which were dear to them" (Hist. Comp. III ,pp 443-444). But it would concur with Pascal that "Although (reason) may be the most sublime of all our faculties it participates nevertheless in the condition of human weakness: everything shows us the state of dependence in which we are placed" (Hist. comp., III, p. 189). In its secular context, Degérando's final position is in no way antipathetic to Pascal's dramatic exposition of the interplay of dogma and doubt. He concludes: "Scepticism and Dogmatism fell into the two excesses of discouragement and presumption; the latter built without reflecting, the former destroyed beyond remedy . . . The philosophy of experience places doubt beside affirmation in order to guard it and not to become its enemy" (Hist. comp., III, p. 569).

The earlier edition of the *Histoire comparée* suggests that Degérando's introduction to Pascal had been made through the Condorcet edition; the corrected and amplified 1847 edition refers to the 1817 edition of the *Pensées* by Didot. The twenty pages devoted to Pascal in this new study indicate both a more understanding attitude on the part of the author and the maturing of his own notions with reference to those of the seventeenth-century apologist. He is among the first to discover in Pascal's scientific genius the sources of his rigorous demonstrations of religious truths: "He had become accustomed, in the process of his mathematical observations, to develop a need for the absolute which the conditions of scientific philosophy could not answer" *(Hist. comp.* 1847 ed., VII, p. 146). Degérando is unwilling to relinquish reason in favor of dogma. He criticizes Pascal for failing to recognize the necessity for philosophy to attempt its tentative hypotheses on the nature of time, space and matter. He finds two men in Pascal, one who observes and reflects on the meaning of life with a "fair and just mind," and another who is committed to a doctrine and who would turn everything "to the interest of the system." It is no easy matter for an enlightened product of eighteenth-century philosophy to grant an unbiased hearing to the exponent of dogmatic religion. But Degérando recognizes in the life of Pascal a harmonious balance which could only exist if the doctrine were healthy. He observes that of the two men existing in Pascal, "each has reached his goal," and that in spite of the limitations which his religion imposed on him, "few men have contributed so much, either to give reason a deserved confidence in itself or to assign at the same time a wise direction to its efforts" *(Hist. comp.,* VII, p. 158). Damiron has suggested that if Degérando had not composed his history of philosophy at a time when ideology had won a dominant position in the intellectual world, his conclusions would have been quite different. Analytical studies of the origin of thought were simply not enough to stir his imagination, and it is Pascal more than any other who succeeds in accomplishing this task.

A VICTORY FOR PASCAL. In Degérando's last philosophical publication, *Du perfectionnement moral* (1826), the full cycle of the evolution of the *philosophy of experience* from Condillac to Pascal is visible. His reservations about Christianity have fallen. With Pascal he asks: "What is life other than a vast desire and a long await-ing?" Undoubtedly the recent death of Maine de Biran and the lat-ter's acceptance of Christianity have had their effect on Degérando. The style in which this combination of personal experience and philo-sophical meditation is expressed could only come from an intimate ac-quaintance with the *Pensées*, as he conlcudes: "Among all living be-ings, only man knows the limit, the too short limit of his days; he sees in advance the grave open to receive him . . ." *(Du perf. mor.,* I, p. 161). Indeed, Christianity is presented as the greatest known force for moral perfection. It alone has synthesized the love of good-ness and the mastery of self which had previously been treated sepa-rately by the classical moralists. In a concluding passage the author, always something of an eclectic, reviews the various forms of Chris-tian apology which we have already noted in the works of Joseph de Maistre, as well as the social theories of the Christian liberals and Pascal's definition of the duality of human nature. It is the religion of Pascal which gives Degérando the theme of his book:

> (Christianity) has been on earth the most powerful promoter of moral perfection, because it has loosened the intellect from the chains of the senses, the heart from the bonds of passion, without misunderstanding any of the conditions and demands of our na-ture; because it has made the essence of religion consist of this per-fection itself. *Du perf. mor.* I, p. 449.

Pascal did not find an easily satisfied audience among early nine-teenth-century philosophers. In the case of Degérando his letter of introduction was his contribution to the sciences. His concept of the progress of scientific knowledge, of the intuitive nature of first principles and of the application of the method of geometry to the demonstrations of logic exert an appeal on the eclectic mentality which is looking for more deeply-rooted grounds for faith in the operations of nature than those provided by rationalism. The era of Voltaire had successfully demolished the claims of revealed religion, but the apparent "crimes" which rationalism had committed in the process provoked a new awareness of the need for a more dynamic, inner-centered ethics than the utilitarianism of the materialists. Degérando is not the only member of the new generation to seek in Pascal's notion of the "heart" a more intimate and profound basis for moral action. Coupled with the work of Maine de Biran, this development of ideology is one of the most striking and enduring segments of nineteenth-century thought.

A CRITICAL REVIEW. The critics have dealt harshly with the schools of ideology and eclecticism.

It is true that the major philosophical productions of this period in France did not impose a system of thought nor create major landmarks in the history of ideas. A contemporary of most of the thinkers whom we have examined, Damiron, sums up the very cautious attitude of the philosophy of his day in his history of contemporary thought: "Philosophizing is no more than travelling for the truth. Will you travel without finding out whether anyone before you had tried the same enterprise and what countries have been recognized, what countries partially seen, poorly identified or poorly described?"[6] As might be expected, such a thoroughly planned and documented expedition might well never get out of port, and even then would never plunge daringly into uncharted seas. On the other hand, a philosophy conducted by these principles might very well play a useful part in the long course of intellectual exploration. It could provide a time for weighing and measuring, a time for maturing and a time for evaluating those positions established in the past.

This is exactly the contribution made by post-revolutionary philosophy in France: it avoided excesses and it brought the past into focus. At a time when Bentham and Mill in England and Schelling in Germany were carrying the themes of individualism and liberty to their extreme limits, the French were concerned with repairing the results of unlimited individualism during the Revolution and with preventing the excesses of repression under Napoleon and the Restoration. Even the most conservative of the academic philosophers, Royer-Collard, was willing to sacrifice his career when his hoped-for constitutional monarchy failed to provide public freedoms. It would seem that their unwillingness to champion any extreme social doctrine was paralleled by an inability to defend any systematic philosophical thesis. They appeared to suffer a philosophical *mal de siècle* which paralyzed their wills at the thought of creating a new society or a new idea. Yet they were men of great dignity and personal idealism. The *Leçons* of Laromiguière uplifted and inspired a generation of philosophers, and it was perfectly consistent with his thought that Degérando should present Maine de Biran's son, as a wedding gift, with a subsidy for the education of two blind persons. Philosophers of this sort will have their moments of elevation, but never of illumination or fanaticism.

In their scrutiny of the past, ideologists and eclectics were looking for three things: a reasonable basis for spiritualistic doctrines which had been too long neglected, an intuitive principle which would underlie physical phenomena and permit man to know the world by knowing himself, and finally an ethical system which would sustain individual morality where the rationalistic principles of the revolution seemed to have failed. Moralists like Rivarol and Degérando were limited in their search for these objectives by their deep-seated prejudice against all the documents of Christianity. Yet each philosopher came under the spell of Pascal and was deeply influenced by him. The spiritualism of the eclectics is clearly a modification of Pascal's contention that Christianity is true because it alone accounts for the dualism of human nature. The intuitive principle which ideology sought was found in his exposition of the axiom that "first principles are sensed, propositions must be proved." And the ethical system which emerged triumphant from the cautious probings of eclectics and ideologists alike was the one derived from the "heart" of Pascal: one in which moral action is possible not because the world functions by physical laws, but because man can attain inner knowledge of God. In Rivarol's *Discours préliminaire* and Degérando's final version of the *Histoire comparée*, this discovery alone opens up new perspectives for the future and inspires the hesitant but sincere movement into the field of moral philosophy of men who were themselves incapable of complete dedication to any exclusive doctrine.

PHILOSOPHICAL BACKGROUND. The high crest of optimism which carried forward the eighteenth century culminated in the loss of self, the loss of religious meaning and the death of Cartesian rationalism at the hands of one of its own children, empiricism. With Descartes, the self possessed an inner reality, whose nature was that of thought, related through intuition to God and nature. The subsequent deductive systems of Spinosa and Leibnitz arrived at the logical conclusion that, as an intuited reality, nature must also be of the same spiritual essence as the self. Traditional western dualism and flourishing empiricism would permit no such dissipation of the physical, extended world of objects. So if the world could not be interpreted in terms of self, the eighteenth century would pursue the notion of Locke that the self might be explained in terms of the world. In the hands of Hume this would make of the self a disconnected series of phenomena, originating in the world of objects and lacking any observable causal sequences. French empiricism was no more successful: for Condillac the self never became more than the localized scene of sensations flowing from the world through a complex receptacle. Accretions might mount up in the receptacle in the form of ideas, but no reality emerged with any of the independent characteristics which might serve to identify a legitimate self. On the phenomenological level, Kant concurred with Hume. It was left for the post-Revolutionary philosopher, like Maine de Biran, to devote his life to the search for a metaphysical self within the range of experimental verification.

Eighteenth-century ethics were unable to develop much beyond the "natural morality" of Shaftsbury. "Nature, for him, is a vast system of interconnected and interdependent parts, of which we see little, but enough to be convinced that it is an admirable Cosmos, moving majestically according to unalterable laws."[7] This carefully arranged, English garden of a universe was uncomfortably close to Leibnitz' "best of all possible worlds," but even the critical Voltaire could find no serious cause for pessimism about the ends of creation at the conclusion of his most devastating attack on religious optimism and teleology in *Candide*. What, then, became of ethical motivation? At its weakest point it expressed Holbach's cheerful notion of self-interest: "That progress would take place as a consequence of man's tendency to advance his own position."[8] The most appealing formula was Rousseau's intimate "sense of conscience," but even this was subjected to considerations of political expediency. Finally, the specter of Hume constantly called into question the very freedom of volition on which individual morality must be based. By identifying morality with the mechanical laws of nature or with external social evolution, the *philosophes* permitted the sense of self-involvement in ethical demands to decline. The loss was not immediately noticed because of the previous disappearance of both the historical and phenomenological self.

NEW SOURCES: KANT AND BIRAN. Immanuel Kant is generally credited with bridging the gap between eighteenth and nineteenth-century philosophy. By his demonstration "that it is the mind that gives laws to nature," he provides the nineteenth-century realists with an answer to Hume's scepticism. By his reservation that "These laws . . . do not go beyond experience," he carries empiricism over into nineteenth-century pragmatism. But Kant continues to deal with the problems of philosophy on the rational or logical grounds of the eighteenth century. Moral freedom, for example, is not the quality which living beings feel in their actions, but the "Property of the Will of all Rational Beings."[9] Kant leads us to human experience, but he does not hold us there.

In reality the firmest thread of continuity between the two centuries turned out to be the methodology of empiricism, particularly in the emerging biological sciences. Lamarck (1744-1829), in his research on invertebrates, suggests new possibilities of the origins of species which will be elaborated by Darwin. Tracy and Doctor Cabanis turn to the physiology of the mind and suggest distinctions between conscious and unconscious volition that will be given further development by Freud. Finally, this new portrait of man is grasped in a full metaphysical sense by Maine de Biran, whose philosophy became a major source of Bergson's system of intuition.

In the philosophy of Maine de Biran, body and soul are caught in the act of living. A dynamic self is discovered, incapable of further atomization by rational analysis. Reason ceases to appear as an isolated phenomenon, opposed to matter or passion. Instead, it becomes an emergent factor of human experience: a stage in the development of the human organism. By clinging obstinately to the techniques of observation and analysis, Biran helps to keep alive the scientific method. By applying it to the mind itself, he gives science a new scope which has not yet been fully exploited. By remaining sensitive to metaphysical questions, his observations on the nature of the religious experience appear for perhaps the first time in conjunction with the procedures of modern psychology. In Biran's progress from the empirical discovery of self to that of faith we find the fullest flow of post-revolutionary thought and the beginnings of the modern existentialist confrontation of being.

Animal Life and Fatality

For the first fifteen years of his philosophical research Maine de Biran is largely interested in the organic determinations of human behavior. His earliest themes, therefore, are "animal life" on the philosophical level and "fatality" on the ethical. From the diverse and subtle ways in which he approaches these themes, he has been variously labelled another Epictetus, a Montaigne, a Pascal, a Rousseau.[10] It is especially important to clarify Biran's relationship to his sources and the original sense of his early themes, as he is so careful and methodical a thinker that he will not leave an idea until it has yielded all its dimensions. His later consideration of the "life of man" and the 'life of the spirit" stand firmly rooted in the facts which had been established at the very beginning. There is in Maine de Biran an enthusiastic seeker of truth, a metaphysician listening for the harmony of the spheres, but one who will never turn his back on humble origins rooted in organic existence. So we shall begin at the foundations of Biran's "living philosophy."

ETHICAL SOURCES. Biran's philosophy begins with an apparently irreconcilable thirst for moral freedom and self-control and a deep awareness of the physical factors determining his actions. He is a plaything of nature: "sad or happy, calm or agitated according to the temperature of the air, according to my good or bad digestion," and yet: "I am intimately convinced that there can be no happiness for me without proper conduct in conformity with the true principles of morality."[11] His readings at this time, drawing heavily on the moralists of the seventeenth and the sensationalists of the eighteenth century, do nothing to resolve his dilemma.

Biran's reflections on human psychology are influenced by Condillac's derivation of consciousness from sensation and by Bonnet's *Essai analytique sur l'Ame,* in which ideas are conceived to be the products of the interplay of brain fibers. His critical attitudes are formed in the main stream of ideology. In one of his final writings he still identifies the "true principle" of philosophy as the conception that thought "is the expression of inner sense, not of metaphysical notion."[12] Life appears much more a physical than a spiritual phenomenon. His only point of departure for the time being is an ethical interest in volition in place of the more epistemological and sociological concerns of his sources. So he suggests that "it would be very desirable that a man accustomed to observing himself should analyse the will as Condillac has analysed the understanding."[13] Moreover, Condillac, in the tradition of Locke, tended to treat mind as a sort of reproduction of the exterior realities of nature. Not only is Biran more interested in a more personal area, that of volition, he is also conscious of an exclusively inner network of organic determinations: "I conceive that for a certain state of the body there always corresponds a certain state of mind." He is fully launched, then, as an ideologist of the soul, a methodical seeker for inward realities. His observations will be those of an intensely introspective philosopher upon his own organic and moral life.

At the same moment Maine de Biran is devouring the writings of the great ethical thinkers with ardent enthusiasm, but with the wavering allegiances of a neophyte in search of a master. Many of his moods are caught up from Rousseau. His situation and character enlist him naturally among the "promeneurs solitaires." From Rousseau he has drawn a notion of virtue which is impotent in "our miserable world," and which drives us on to "an imaginary and better world."[14] Biran has also tasted the early fruits of disillusionment with the enlightenment. His imagination is impelled backwards in history or inwards to self; it cannot bear the cold, demanding present. With Rousseau he yearns for a past Golden Age: "for just as in antiquity one had reasons to develop one's soul and become man, so in our days everything restricts, everything tarnishes our corrupt generation."[15] His religious feeling is expressed as the unformulated theism inspired by the Savoyard Vicar and oriented by nature: "I am studying in myself what is the true happiness to which nature invites us and I thank the Being who made me as I am."

But if the tone is Rousseauistic, the method is more reminiscent of Montaigne. It consists, at this time, of unorganized observations of the perpetual flux of inner states of mind: "I often amuse myself by watching the flow of the various situations of my soul; they are like the currents of a river, now calm, now agitated, but always following each other without any permanence." Like the sceptical observer of the tumultuous sixteenth century, Biran professes to pursue detachment and inner peace and recommends for this a healthy physical regimen. In the best Lucretian manner he points out that "we would not be long in discovering that moderation in everything. . . . the pleasures attached to a pure conscience and good health could alone lead us to that physical condition in which I conceive happiness to exist." In fact, he does not ignore the siren call of Epicurus himself and pays tribute to the philosopher who understood the true nature of man and who wished to "scatter flowers" in the path of duty and "transform duties into pleasures."[16] With a slightly more critical eye he consults Pascal and the stoics. He suspects the latter of a streak of masochism. He is in complete accord with Pascal concerning the misery of the human condition, but questions the conclusion that the explanation lies with original sin: "Is man no more than a degenerate being, or is he destined for a greater perfection?"[17]

It is clear that Maine de Biran is disposed to evaluate human nature on physical grounds and that his early ethical penchant is towards the primrose path. It would be wrong, however, to attach theoretical values to the details of these earliest investigations. Biran is testing the field of philosophy with wide-ranging interest and elasticity of mind. Everything that he reads becomes his by assimilation into the marrow of his emotions. He is now ready to undertake one of the most personal and creative philosophical journeys of his times.

THE SUBCONSCIOUS DEPTHS. As a thoroughgoing ideologist in the manner of Condillac, Bonnet and Cabanis, Biran adopts an attitude of complete physical determinism. In one of the many pre-Freudian insights he discloses that the roots of human behavior lie hidden away in childhood and in the powerful motivations of the instincts and organic dispositions and habits. Reason thus loses its privileged position. In accordance with mechanism he suggests that animals and children are endowed with no higher form of life than a "sensitive soul" which responds to the urgings of the outer world and in some way adapts the organic system to the requirements of the situation. This sensitized machinery, in fact, is the great teacher of man: "it creates all the first experiences for him, and reflection plays no role in this first education until the organs have reached their degree of perfection."[18] Here is the base on which all of Biran's later insights are superimposed; he will never deny the importance of physiological determinations in the creation of personality and the self.

Since he is constantly on the lookout for the possibilities of self-determination through volition, it does not take Biran long to identify the inadequacies of Condillac's sensualism. In his *Logique* (Chapter VIII), Condillac believed that he had reduced epistemology to an algebraic system in which unknown quantities of sensations could be traced from the known elements in the body of knowledge. As Biran was frequently to point out, if man were no more than a closed system of sensations, he would be knowledge, he would not possess it. At some point an awareness must arise distinguishing between the objects of sensation and the sensing subject. Destutt de Tracy attempted to overcome the lacuna by identifying the subject with the capacity for movement. The self would thus be identified by the process of elimination as that movement which was found to have no external source of motion. In his earliest writings Biran attributes the consciousness of *self* to the fact of volition:

"If the individual did not *wish,* or was not determined to begin to move, he would know nothing. If nothing resisted him, he would not know anything either, he would not suspect any existence, he would not even have an idea of his own."[19]

An "experienced" dualism accounts for Biran's unique and seminal role in nineteenth-century philosophy. In the *Mémoire sur l'habitude* he suggests the distinction which Bergson will later exploit between voluntary and involuntary memory. In this debut before the public Biran presents the principle of life as a force "which maintains several intimate movements in the organized whole which it animates."[20] These movements are the involuntary habits in which our existence is grounded. Unlike Bergson, Biran does not pursue the elusive principle of life. He is content with the empirical task of observing the effects of this underground life and with distinguishing them from those of the "motive force" rising from the conscious volition of the subject. While the former are always buried below the level of consciousness, the latter are "not subjected to the same law nor the same modes of degeneracy"; they may be saved in the act of recollection. Here Biran distinguishes between a "mechanical memory" involving the simple repetition of movements (Bergson locates these more precisely in various intermediary nerve centers), the voluntary recall of an intellectual symbol by the "representative memory," and the recall of an affective or emotional symbol in "sensitive memory."[21] From the empirical data furnished by Biran in support of his thesis to the re-examination of subjective and objective time is a relatively short step which will be made by Proust and Bergson.

The vital theme which most clearly reveals the development of Biran as a major modern philosopher is that of causality. As an empiricist he is greatly influenced by Hume's critique of the notions of identity and causality. In his early works he frequently depicts man as a successive being, not a continuous flow of any constant experience. He attempts to locate a causal self, an identity, in the memory (Tisserand, Vol. I, p. 239), but this fails to answer Hume's argument that if self is located in conscious memory we are faced with its dissolution in unconsciousness and its mysterious resurgence with the return of consciousness. In the *Mémoire sur l'habitude* he appears to acquiesce to Hume. He observes that even those actions initiated by the motive force of the subject soon pass into the conditioning of the organism and disappear from consciousness. These acquired habits relieve us from the effort of renewed volition and account for the "false assumption of *essentiality* in habitually simultaneous impressions, and of causality in the familiar order of successive impressions" (Tiss., Vol. II, p. 304). Further examination of the active elements of perception, in the *Mémoire sur la décomposition de la pensée,* will lead to a radically new concept.

The *self* which Kant would preserve from the impermanency of phenomenal existence by placing it among the *noumena* becomes an ethical abstraction. It can be brought to life only by some leap into being such as was taken by Kierkegaard and Heidegger. Biran's *self* is the energy deployed from a common center over the same organism which experienced the stimuli of the physical world as sensation. The experience of effort "is the consciousness of the *self as cause,* and here we are dealing with cause in its simple and individual meaning, the cause which . . . comprehends itself by reflection on its own existence and action."[22] It is defined existentially. It arises from "animal life" at the moment when volition invades the muscles and encounters the resistance of inertia. It is experienced organically, as the physical world is experienced; its effects may be isolated by the brain and it may thus be known. But this would not be the conceptual knowledge of rationalism: "the apperception of *self* is always founded on an act, or the result of an act, which is a very real mode, and not at all a pure abstract concept."[23] With this discovery of a self quantitatively present as a positive polarity of the human organism, Biran feels that he has exposed the "very archetype" of the absolute by which we may know the categories by which the absolute is expressed, such as "causality, identity, unity and plurality." In anticipation of Freud, Biran has perceived in man a total economy of being, active and passive, dynamic and receptive. Where Freud identifies the energy sources with the "underground life," Biran conceives the physical being of man as the meeting-place of animal drives and some "hyper-organic force" whose action is evident in conscious volition.

Here Biran establishes the limits of "animal life": at the moment of the discovery of the "other life" of the self, the "life of man." It is the animal life to which man is born and which brings him to the degree of organic sophistication from which consciousness may emerge. The moral level of animal life is fatality. The term "fatum" comes more frequently to Biran as he discovers contrasting areas of human freedom and finally of divine "inclination." He has found the philosophical equivalent of the helplessness which he expressed in the early years of the *Diary*: the impossibility of living beyond the physical events which held him in slavery. In his final work, the *Nouveaux essais d'Anthropologie*, he still refers to animal existence as enclosed in "this fatal circle," but by then the circle has been broken: "the active and free being, man alone, passes beyond; and the beginning of his life of relation or of consciousness opens to him a career of moral development which should have no other barriers than his own activity."[24] Too many of Biran's critics fail to recognize that his empiricism is an autobiographical empiricism. His convictions never overreach what he has observed or experienced within himself. His philosophical account of human liberty and divine grace is therefore a curious combination of personal warmth and scientific objectivity. Biran's classical moderation is quite unique at a time when the violence of public events led many thinkers to positions of emotional extremes. It is derived, perhaps, like that of Sophocles, from a sense of the union in man of the subterranean forces of destiny and the vital energy of the individual human spirit.

The life of man — Freedom.

THE WILL. There is no theme which distinguishes the philosophic attitude of the eighteenth century from that of the nineteenth more clearly than that of volition and the nature of human freedom. It is interesting that the English empiricists and philosophers whose works established the claims for civil liberties should think of man as the product of external conditioning factors in his moral and psychological life. In his excellent study Hallie shows that Hume and Locke consider human freedom at best to exist in the absence of external obstacles. Hume therefore concludes that "man never has liberty, for he is always involved in a causal sequence."[25] Biran would object that causality is a mode of experience, not a logical necessity: that it is perceived in our role as agent. Locke, on the other hand defines cause as *"That which produces any simple or complex idea."*[26] It is therefore external to volition and can only be derived by reason as a necessary antecedent to the perceived idea. Man, according to Locke, is therefore not a moral *agent*, but a moral *being*. He is capable of knowing the moral situation, but not of creating it. John Gay provides a clear illustration of the way in which this concept of the "ethical idea" passes into the ethics of utilitarianism when he suggests that: "Though it be necessary in order to solve the principal actions of human life to suppose a moral sense. . . . and also public affections; yet I deny that this moral sense, or these public affections are innate or implanted in us. They are acquired either from our own observation or the imitation of others."[27] Moral determinations, being external to the self, thereby pass into the hands of society which will become practically the *ens causa sui* of the ethics of Bentham and Mill.

Much of the same atmosphere of moral determinism prevailed in France. Together with a tenacious optimism in the capacities of human reason, there flows an equally strong current of sceptical fatalism. Diderot proved a devoted partisan of the enlightenment in the compilation of the *Encyclopedia*. Yet in *Rameau's Nephew,* among more cynical observations, he notes that: "To whatever man applies himself, it is nature who designed him for it."[28] There is an even more curious juxtaposition of inner determinism and outward freedom in two articles of the *Dictionnaire philosophique*. In the first, *On Liberty,* Voltaire proves that freedom could be nothing more than "the power that your person has used to do what your will commanded. . ."[29] Volition is not a causal factor in human experience, however, since other motivations can be shown to precede and condition the act of volition. In a hypothetical situation Voltaire imagines that B supposes that he *wishes* to marry. The wish is not a free act, since it can be shown that it is based upon a previously acquired love for the girl in question. Voltaire concludes triumphantly: "You see that you cannot will without a reason." With Locke, Voltaire contends that: "Your will is not free, but your actions are." The resulting high value which is placed on external freedom becomes evident in the following article on the "Freedom of Thought." Here the author develops one of his favorite themes: the removal of obstacles to the free, public interplay of ideas. Freedom as a quality of self-determination is an imaginative fiction. True freedom for the *philosophe* is a relational term between the individual and society. It consists in the absence of impediments to the physical, economic or intellectual actions of the individual. It is won or lost on the political rather than the spiritual field of battle.

In its general outlines nineteenth-century philosophy reversed this definition of freedom. Among thinkers of the French romantic period this takes the form of a sense of loss. Like exiles from the paradise of reason, Senancour, Constant, Musset and Vigny feel the tragic sense of a vitiated, inadequate will, the *mal de siècle*. There is no hope now from society. On the contrary, Saint-Simon, Hegel, Comte and Spencer will identify society as the product of the inevitable laws of history and it is now sociological freedom which appears fictitious. At the same time volition is discovered to underly the "free act." Schopenhauer derives from Kant the "noumenal will" which is free as an unconditioned identity. Projected into the world of phenomena, this "noumenal will" becomes limited and thereby conditioned. But it is free as an act expressing a unique existence: "Therefore every man is what he is through his original will, and knowledge merely leads him to learn in the course of experience *what he is,* i.e., his character, from which his particular acts of will follow with necessity."[30] By combining this interpretation of volition as an unbounded affirmation of existence and the sterile, mechanistic universe into which it may be projected, Nietzsche arrives at his "will to power." As hope for Utopia fades, man's thirst for freedom turns inward, this time not for moral inspiration but rather in a desperate effort to preserve the green shoots of being from the withering blasts of logic and legality.

As we have observed, Maine de Biran is fully conscious of the many elements which determine human behavior. His response, however, leads neither to scientific mechanism nor to excessive voluntarism. He points the way rather to the naturalism and pragmatism of the late nineteenth and early twentieth centuries, to intuitionism and to the existentialism of Husserl and Jaspers. Like the post-Comptian naturalist he depicts human life as emerging from the basic elements of nature, not the invasion of nature by a foreign "soul substance."[31] For Bergson this "surge of life" constitutes the primitive fact of reality and human knowledge is merely the reduction of intuition into symbols.

In the same way for Biran, science stems from the original intuition of self. It then traces two separate lines as it pursues the active and passive elements of the original intuition: "Those two points of view (physical and psychological) of the science of the same living being, feeling and willing or acting, are founded on the essential distinction established previously between the faculties of intuition and immediate apperception, to which the two groups of external and internal facts correspond respectively."[32] So the *self* which emerges in the sense of effort as distinct from its phenomenal origins shows the quality of freedom in the newly created "life of man." "In becoming aware of its existence, its individual force, the *self* may consider its force or power for acting, as the model. . . of all force or power. . . ."[33] This process of universalizing the experience of individual existence is precisely the function of reason according to Jaspers: "The decision for Reason — which is also a decision for freedom, truth and unconditionality of existential decision — is against nature, occurrence and necessity. One can call it the Unnatural as opposed to the 'innocence of nature.' "[34] In his philosophical studies from 1813 to 1817 Biran has found in the analysis of volition a description of the human condition which is to be deeply significant for the twentieth century.

The will underlies Biran's epistemology: it also underlies his metaphysics and his ethics. If we consider man in his position as both the subject and object of movement, we shall recognize the true quality of his dualism: "and we can discover the role of the animal subjected to the fatal laws of a material organization, what that being is that is raised to the rank of an intelligent and moral person by the free activity on which all his preeminence is founded."[35] The dualism is not fundamental, however, it is rather the product of potential points of view. It is reconciled in the intuition which accompanies the sense of effort in willing. Here in the life of man is an absolute, an irreducible reality. Since reason is the instrument by which intuitive knowledge is abstracted and converted into the symbols by which man communicates, Biran refers to reason as "the faculty of the absolute." This conception is found in Biran's works as early as 1813,[36] but he will never formalize it. As the last of three major systems of human nature: affective, representative and reflective, reason provides a minor, structural interest. Coming into play with the act of willing, however, it is doubly important: it attests the existence of the absolute of volition and it provides the symbolized content of moral responsibility.

This existential ground accounts for Biran's opposition to Cartesian idealism. Human will and reason are expressions of unique experience. They do not depend for validity upon a divine will or reason. The Abbé de Lignac suggested that the power for volition was not self-caused and that it must therefore be considered a contingent process depending on the action of God. Biran argues that "the union of body and soul, being enclosed in the inward sense, can be nothing other than the intimate apperception which the motive force has of itself in action on a sensitive or affectible organized body."[37] The first step in Biran's metaphysics therefore is the identification of an experientially-grounded absolute. In conscious volition we are introduced to a "coenesthèse," a totality of sensing, willing and knowing which Biran carefully distinguishes from the animal life of pre-consciousness.

Biran rejects both the empirical and rational notions of the self. He replaces these with a self which is free, causal and morally responsible. Having observed the relationship of the will and reason *in act,* not as metaphysical identities, he concludes that "the repeated exercise of reflection transforms the law of duty into a sort of fortunate necessity which offers the most obvious characteristics of freedom and becomes its most vital sanction."[38] At this point in his development he pauses to examine the philosophical attitudes of his contemporaries. From his studies of Laromiguière's *Leçons de Philosophie* he clarifies the meaning of freedom. Laromiguière contends that freedom is "the power to will or to refrain from willing," that it is "born from desire." Biran responds that volition is not a power, but an activity — a willed action "joined with judgment and reflection." As for desire, it does not act as a cause upon the will. Desire may produce dispositions in the organism, but the will is a faculty and "no faculty is the effect of another faculty although it may follow it in time." It bears its own testimony, "the feeling of freedom. . . to begin a motion without being constrained."[39] From the mechanism of animal life, the life of the self arises in the acts of willing and thinking. This new mode of life, the life of man, stands forth from nature "as an acting force which frees him from the bonds of *fatality* and constitutes him as an individual, moral person, intelligent and free."

This is also the time during which Biran takes an important step toward the future by bringing religion within the "philosophy of experience." He is certainly no theologian, although his studies of the gospel of Saint John during the final days of his life, show skill and deep interest in exegesis. He is quite hostile to the spirit of Bonald and Lamennais, who would define the life of man in terms of religious concept. Of the philosophers of religion he is perhaps most strongly attracted by Leibnitz. The latter's dynamic spiritualism, suggesting that "beings are forces," appeals to Biran's interpretation of volition. From Leibnitz he draws his definition of the soul as "a force, a cause of action, having awareness of itself through its activity." But his concern is ethical, rather than metaphysical. He is interested in the ends of being insofar as they illuminate the condition of man. His final works, including the *Nouveaux Essais d'Anthropologie*, reflect intensive study of the *Pensées* of Pascal. The results of this meditation are felt in his doctrine of the "life of the spirit" and serve to draw Pascal into the main stream of nineteenth-century philosophy.

Life of the spirit — Grace.

With his discovery in volition of an existential mode of human freedom, an absolute causality at the disposal of self, Biran also encountered the reef on which many existentialists foundered: the problem of responsibility. Nietzsche encloses his answer within the self by raising the self to ultimate reality and by placing in its hands a super-will. But we are led to wonder whether Nietzsche has described a super man or a minor monster. Ibsen's Oswald Alving found for himself the "joy of life," the existential freedom, but his petulant egotism suggests no particularly fruitful goal for the "liberated personality." In fact, the slave to the conventions of society, Mrs. Alving, speaks much more warmly to us than does her self-willed, free-spirited son. In 1816 Biran was tempted to formulate an ethical theory based upon the exclusive powers of the will: "The will must preside over all that we are: that is stoicism. No other system is so suitable to our nature."[40] Within a few years, however, his investigations of the "third life" lead him to conclude that the ethic of stoicism is "above the forces of humanity." "Christianity alone embraces the whole of man. . . by showing him all the need which he has of help from a higher source."[41] He has found that human life is a pulsation between two poles, the physical and the spiritual. It is the moment of freedom won from nature, but it is also the moment of truth, in which the passionate affirmation of self-existence is touched by the spirit of God and directed to a morality which could never be "created" by the self.

The third part of Biran's *Nouveaux Essais d'Anthropologie*, the *Vie de l'Esprit*, falls into two main divisions: one describing the condition of man without God and the other dealing with divine love. The first objective is precisely that of Pascal, and Biran adapts the *Pensées* with familiarity and conviction. The psychology of loss for which Chateaubriand found a lyrical expression comes through as basic human experience in Biran: "and those who abandon themselves the most completely to the animal life are often more tormented by the demands of another nature, which are expressed in uneasiness, boredom, inward agitation which torment the unfortunates outwardly endowed with the most brilliant gifts of fortune or nature: *"All creatures tremble."*[42] Man without God is unfinished, his will is a vain pawing at the air: "To escape the abyss, he must find a support outside himself." Impelled outwards by the incompleteness of his humanity, man encounters the true end of being in God. The contact is pragmatic, as undeniable as the consciousness of effort at the beginning of willed action. It is experienced, but it is beyond the level of conceptualization. It is like the relationship of "persons united closely by the bonds of love and friendship, (who) have no need to talk in order to understand each other, to be content together." This silent, supra-rational touching of divinity will be given further development by William James and Martin Buber. We shall see the decisive role of Pascal in its formulation.

The tone of the *Nouveaux Essais* differs from Biran's earlier works by the feeling of completion and finality which distinguishes it from the painstaking observations and tentative hypotheses of the latter. The reason is that the author has completed the cycle from the physiology of the senses to the psychology of the religious impulse. He had previously identified the organic conditions which set the fundamental tone of physical experience. He had described the thrust of the causal self against these determinations in the acts of willing and reasoning. He is now conscious of a third source of energy and motivation: religious belief. Human freedom operates within verifiable limits. Without recourse to the mechanisms of nature we cannot cure illness and insanity. For moral energy and motivation, the rational self cannot be expected to frustrate its own ego-preserving function. At this point "religion comes to his aid," by furnishing the material from which ethical desires are derived and sustained and by ending the impossible search for finality within the scope of the active self.

Boutroux accuses both Maine de Biran and William James of failing to establish that the proposition: "I feel divine activity in me" is identical with the proposition: "Divine activity takes place in me." This, however, is to misunderstand the limits placed on philosophical speculation by Biran and James. For Biran the function of philosophy is to distinguish the various components of the human experience and to define its limits. The limit of affirmative statement is to be found within the action of will and reason. To go beyond is to enter the ethical or ideal environment in which the self must be submerged beneath higher values and resume the role of instrument rather than the goal of action. The history of human reason for Biran culminates in the discovery of this ideal environment and the will finds its ultimate purpose in directing the self to the conditions of ideality. Having verified in his own experience the modifications brought about through religious belief, Biran is justified in observing the relationship of his belief to his character. He does not claim to have described the object of belief, merely its appearance as motivation in the subject. Biran would agree with Santayana that to penetrate beyond these limits is to enter the field of poetic or religious imagination. Biran correctly senses here the completion of his psychological empiricism.

ROLE OF PASCAL. Biran's interest in Pascal extends over the entire period of his mature intellectual life. The relationship is sufficiently deep to provide a distinct field of study for the main critics of Biran and is the subject of A. de la Valette-Monbrun's volume, *Maine de Biran, critique et disciple de Pascal*. Interpretation of the relationship ranges from Tisserand's opinion that "while with Pascal philosophy is subordinated to religion which alone can enlighten him, M. de Biran makes faith bend before reason and identifies the true religion with philosophy," to Valette-Monbrun's thesis that the "three lives" of Biran are the direct descendants of the "three orders of truth" of Pascal.[43] We shall attempt to follow only the clear lines of Biran's development as he tests Pascalian doctrine in his search for an authentic conclusion to his own unique combination of induction and intuition. There are probably few generalizations which would have greater justification than one to the effect that Pascal discovered man in his search for God while Biran found God in his search for man. This is a study of the interpenetration of the ways.

From 1815 to 1818 Biran became increasingly interested in the philosophy of the *Pensées*, culminating in 1817 and 1818 with the detailed analyses of the *Notes of Voltaire and Condorcet on the Pensées of Pascal*. For most of this time Biran is hostile to Pascal. The latter is suspected of being blindly committed to a preconceived system. Pascal's definition of *ennui* and his vision of man's need to live beyond himself is seen as superficial propaganda to demonstrate the results of original sin and "make a complete abstraction of the influence of his organic and sensitive condition on the feeling which he has of his existence."[44] Before 1817 Biran is concerned with describing human freedom, the rights and privileges of the self. He is therefore uncomfortable when faced by Pascal's notion of the nothingness of human existence without God. He complains that "when, like Pascal, one regrets being entertained by frivolous objects, it is as though one regretted being a man."

Le Roy accurately summarizes the extent of these early criticisms as "signifying that the mistake of Pascal was to invoke a theological explanation where a simpler, psychological explanation was needed."[45] But for Maine de Biran the life of philosophy is a total project in the free pursuit of truth. So in May of 1823 we find Biran reflecting on the *pensée*: "It is one of the marvels of the Christian religion to reconcile man with himself by conciliating him with God." He recalls that at one time he had found a human completeness in solitude by himself: "But age, the habit of the distractions of the world and its affairs have destroyed this happy *inner temperament*, and I feel now the truth of that whole article by Pascal."[46] This is how the lived religion of Pascal becomes mirrored in the lived philosophy of Maine de Biran.

Until the final phase of his thought, Biran condemns Pascal and Christian theology for their failure to recognize and explain the freedom of the human will. Even in 1817 he is repelled by "that religious belief that man can do nothing by himself, but only by the grace of God."[47] In all of Biran's philosophy, the human experience emerges as a whole, integrating process. In an evening's friendly argument with the abbé Morellet in November of 1817, Biran defended the unity of the self. Morellet had asked Biran to define the self; Biran replied: "We must place ourselves at the intimate point of view of consciousness and, having thus present that unity which judges all phenomena, while remaining unchangeable, we perceive the *self*; we do not ask what it is." Since the *self* is noumenal, a primitive cause, the religious factor can serve as nothing more than an external condition, and the role of grace becomes irreconcilable with the consciousness of self-determination present in the act of volition. Biran is aware of the inadequacy of the self as a moral absolute; he suspects that fulfilment can only be achieved by the absorption of the particular will into the divine, "But can that sublime thought absorb the *self*? and if the *self* is absorbed, how will there be thought and freedom?" This is the dilemma with which

Biran is dealing as he attempts to equate the natural, human and divine elements of life.

The *Pensées* contain two replies to the problem raised by Maine de Biran. The first consists of a review of the methods by which man may use his human freedom to move forward to encounter the way of divinity: by the habits of religion, faith, prayer and charity. In a beautiful passage of his introduction to the *Pensées*, Brunschvicg remarks: "(Pascal's) work is, above all, a prayer: it is addressed both to the sinner, that he turn towards God, to God that he should not turn away from the sinner."[48] To this extent the will is free: it may choose or reject the patterns of action which would place it within the sphere of religious meaning. Human causality is affirmed in the possibility of charity and prayer. The second solution of Pascal lies in denying the metaphysical unity of the *self*. As the product of determinations from above and below, from its organic impulses and the aspirations of its spirit, the self must seek its place in reality, in true being, in order to escape the plunge into nothingness. Unity of being lies therefore in the man-God relationship and the act by which it is expressed is love, rather than self-will. For Pascal this truth is found in the essence of Christian doctrine. It is a concept which impresses Biran, but for him it emerges slowly from the raw facts of human psychology, and as he reads Pascal he adapts to his own system the relationship of man to God: "By loving ourselves, we turn from God, as from a body of which each of us is a member, but by knowing ourselves we go towards God, we are led to know Him."[49]

In the final years of the *Journal Intime* and in the *Nouveaux essais* there is ample evidence that Biran has accepted the major positions taken by Pascal. It is illuminating to observe how, without sacrificing any of the hard-won ground of his psychological empiricism, Biran lays the groundwork for Pascalian faith. The first step is a radical modification of the concept of the absolute *self*. In the final rich years of his life he would find peace as the crown of reason. But the terms of peace cannot be written by the rational self, nor conquered by an effort of the will: "When all might be agreeable and harmonious between the active and sensitive faculties which constitute man, there would still remain a superior nature, a third

116

life, which would not be satisfied. . ."[50] Uneasiness invades his own existence and the dry perfection of his intellectual accomplishments fail to give greater fulfilment. Instead of synthesizing, the self becomes a source of irritation, and Biran confesses that "Pascal has accurately described that condition in which man fears nothing so much as to think of himself."[51] On the grounds of experience Biran revises his metaphysics. "What I took for reality, for the true object of science, has no longer to my mind a more than phenomenal value; my point of departure has changed with my dispositions and my moral character." The life of man and of the spirit depend first upon self-knowledge. In this sense the self is the first legitimate object of reason and the source of volition. But there can be no resting here, since the self is not an ultimate reality: there must be a passage beyond reason to the love of God and absorption of the self: "To love, it is essential that the self be forgotten or lost to view, by relating itself to the beautiful, good and perfect being which is its goal."[52]

In the same way Biran adopts a Pascalian attitude to resolve the dilemma of the free will and absorption into divine will. In his conclusion of the *Nouveaux Essais* Biran offers his interpretation of the *pensée:* "We cannot love what is outside ourselves."[53] Like Pascal, Biran addresses himself to a God whose being penetrates the upper levels of human existence. He is the reality which can be approached through effort and prayer: "He comes only where the way is prepared for Him, He illumines only the senses disposed to receive his impression: such is the use of our activity." Human freedom and moral responsibility therefore acquire purposefulness because they may lead to God, yet they do not lie beyond the reach of common experience. The aspiration to union with God is the final achievement of "the life of man," but the religious, or mystic, experience depends upon an energy which is not of human derivation. It is a release from moral tensions, a love without passion. It is an intuition "by which one sees the truth without seeking. . . , by which one scorns all human knowledge, finding oneself higher than that." Biran does not interpose his own imagination in this account of the mystic experience, but draws heavily from Fénelon, Saint Augustine and Saint John the Evangelist. The framework of his religi-

117

ous philosophy is clearly informed by the spirit of Pascal, the content is based upon the accounts of the mystics, but the point of view remains adamantly personal, the closely observed and verified texture of the life of Maine de Biran.

An endless debate has raged over the debt which Biran's "three lives" owes to the "three orders" of Pascal. Valette-Monbrun asserts that: "The *animal life*, first aspect by which Biran conceives our humanity, corresponds exactly to what Pascal calls the order of matter or nature. Equally, the *human life* corresponds to the order of thought and the *life of the spirit* or of grace to the order of charity."[54] Delbos objects that Biran's conception of the third life is not motivated by any concern for salvation and that any similarity is "not by direct imitation, but by the very progress of his philosophic thought as soon as he wished to understand the given and acquired factors of his religious experience." Amoudru concludes that the content of the two systems is alike, "sensation, free activity, communication with God," but that Biran is not confined to a Pascalian outlook, "as in the mystical domain Pascal gives way to Fénelon. . . so, in the field of knowledge, Pascal yields to Malebranche when it is necessary to explain the interaction of these forces." According to Le Roy, "Pascal insisted only on the discontinuity of the three orders. . . the infinite distance which separates them," while Biran accepts the discontinuity of man's ascent to God, "but he adds that this ascending discontinuity does not exclude a continuity, which is established by descent. . . ." Le Roy is not convinced that Pascal is totally devoid of a sense of the flow of intention from God to man, since he adds in a later paragraph: "That these observations might agree without difficulty with the theory of Pascal, no one argues."

Rather than attempting to thread our way through the subleties of previous criticism, we might shed some light on the argument by considering the clear declarations of Biran and Pascal. For Pascal the first two orders (sensual and rational) are not only incomplete, they are essentially degenerate: "Man without grace is but a thing of error, natural and ineffaceable. . . . These two principles of truth, reason and the senses, besides lacking in sincerity, reciprocally delude each other."[55] Since both the inductive and rationalist methods are confined to untrustworthy instruments, the only approach to truth is through faith, the "instrument of God." Faith differs from proof; one human, the other is God's gift. For Pascal the order of charity is the order of truth, it is not to be reached by any thrust of reason or of will, but by an act of faith. Pascal's objective is to quicken the heart to a conviction of the reality of this "supernatural order."

Maine de Biran, as we have seen, attributes a basic mode of reality to each of the "three lives." The unifying theme is not the third life, but rather the life of man. Nature and God are recognized as distinct realities, yet they are not identified by their essential natures. It is in their manner of modifying any given state of being of the *self* that they acquire the status of legitimate objects of science and belief. So we discover that Pascal's study is of human nature while Biran's is of the self. Pascal would reveal the "misery" of the human condition and then redeem it through the religious experience. Biran also shows the dualistic, conflicting motivations of the self, with a corresponding sense of moral anguish. Yet in his most Pascalian passages in the *Nouveaux Essais*, he places the Christian explanation of the "third life" before the exposition of human suffering. The explanation of this transposition in argument seems to lie in the fact that Pascal is trying to converge the faculties of belief on the central theme of Christianity, while Biran is merely concerned with demonstrating the unique modifications of the self in the religious experience.

One of the most independent minds of the early nineteenth century, Maine de Biran was never the spokesman for another system of thought, including that of Pascal. He found in Pascal the way to a religious experience which forms the fitting conclusion of a comprehensive philosophy in human psychology. Pascal's order of charity touches Biran's more personal life of the mind, stirring it with a thirst for ultimate reality. The context of this experience is the landscape of the *Pensées* but the movement of the actors is inspired by Biran. In fact, the analytical passages of the last years of Biran's *Diary* provide direct enrichment of his commentaries on the doctrine of Pascal. He is deeply interested in an area of experience largely neglected by Pascal: the acts by which the self prepares to enter communication with divinity. For Biran, the religious experience is a divine response to man's desire: "By thinking, for example, voluntarily and often of the supreme cause on whom we depend, by praying and imploring His help, this very action of praying excites in the soul different feelings of desire, admiration and sympathy which may sometimes exalt the intellectual faculties, sometimes produce those ecstatic states in which faculties of another order seem to develop, raising the soul to that condition which Plato and his school have identified, probably in the light of personal experience." When William James adds the *act of faith* to Biran's *act of desire,* he completes the translation into modern psychology of Pascal's definition of man as a God-seeker. The objective is still the divine reality of Western theology and philosophy, but there is a progressive clarification of our understanding of the seeker as an active, conscious and responsible participant in the process by which the truth is fulfilled.

* * *

We have traced the passage of Pascalian ideas through the Romantic period. In detailed analyses, we have seen them take on a warmer and more personal life after their "trial by fire" in the eighteenth century. Having emerged from the ungentle hands of the rationalists, they have been submitted to the even more critical examination of a period in search of a faith. The strength of the *Pensées* is attested by the increasing admiration which they elicited, culminating in the 1840's with the significant studies of Sainte-Beuve and Vinet, the historic reconstructions of the manuscripts by Cousin and subsequently the Faugère and Havet editions.[56] Miss Eastwood, in *The Revival of Pascal,* demonstrates the way in which the *Pensées* regain their authority after the reign of science in the mid-nineteenth century. Our own study has treated the same phenomenon as it appeared after the "age of reason" and erupted into that reign of science, fertilized by some of the most profound thoughts of the Romantic period.

Notes

[1] *Bulletin de Paris*, An X, 7, pp. 222-225.

[2] Thomas Paine, *Age of Reason* (New York), p. 31.

[3] Charles Frankel, *The Faith of Reason* (New York, 1958), p. 143.

[4] *Descartes Selections*, "Meditations on First Philosophy," ed. (Scribner's) 1927, pp. 120-121.

[5] Emile Bréhier, *Histoire de la philosophie*, II, 1 (Presses Universitaires, 1947), p. 252.

Also Félix Ravaisson, *La philosophie de France*, (Paris, 1868), p. 7.

[6] Quotation of Rousseau by Paul Nourrisson, *J.-J. Rousseau et le Rousseauisme* (Paris, 1903), p. 285.

[7] The relative roles of reason and intuition in the religious system of Rousseau have been debated by Schinz and Masson:

"In spite of all appearances, Rousseau remains in fact a rational philosopher, because the content of his moral feeling, or of his ethical conscience that is to say his moral law—that law which takes its form almost word for word from Christian moral law—rests on an entirely different basis . . . . If there is any coincidence between the details of this rational wisdom and the will of a Christian God, so much the better or so much the worse; that has no importance for the thought of Rousseau." Albert Schinz, *La Pensée de J.-J. Rousseau* (Paris, 1929), pp. 225-226.

"In the degree that Rousseau's conception of nature becomes more inward, his religious thought also becomes more detached from reason. The role of reason has become purely negative. A simple auxiliary in the task of spiritual liberation, it has been particularly useful in breaking down the barriers which separate the soul from nature; and, giving complete security to feeling, it has permitted feeling to declare its complete supremacy: 'All our reason', as Pascal said, 'comes down to yielding to feeling'." Pierre Masson, *La Religion de Rousseau*, II, (Paris, 1916), p. 292.

It is true that some of Pascal's concept of the "heart" reappears in Rousseau, thereby passing with certain modifications into the current of nineteenth-century thought. We can only proceed with caution, identifying as precisely as possible the themes and phrases of Pascal and drawing our conclusions from clearly established relationships between the direction of Pascalian feeling and that of Romantic philosophy.

8 Jeremy Bentham, "Principles of Morals and Legislation," in *The English Philosophers from Bacon to Mill* (N.Y. 1939), p. 810.

9 Immanuel Kant, *Metaphysics of Morals* (Chicago, 1949), p. 35.

10 The quotation is taken from J. J. Mounier, *De l'influence attribuée aux philosophes* . . . (Tubingen, 1801), p. 132. For a complete analysis of French Mysticism of this period, see J. Buche, *Ecole mystique de Lyon* (Paris, 1935).

11 Citation taken from E. Dermenghem, *Joseph de Maistre, mystique* (Paris, 1923), p. 59.

12 For the relationship of Robespierre to Rousseau, see Albert Mathiez, *La Révolution et l'Eglise* (Paris, 1910), p. 70. Where Aulard, in *Culte de la Raison,* attributes the violence of the Terror to religious emotions, Mathiez insists on its political nature: "Robespierre opposed the movement (to destroy Christian organizations in France), because its authors, assembled at opposite poles of the political horizon, led the attack both against the Committee of Public Safety and against the Church." p. 146.

13 Albert Monod, *De Pascal à Chateaubriand* (Paris, 1916), p. 499. For other works giving the general background of the material covered in the introduction, but not referred to in footnotes, consult the following: George Boas, *French Philosophies of the Romantic Period* (Baltimore, 1925).

Emile Cailliet, *La Tradition Littéraire des Idéologues* (Philadelphia, 1943).

Victor Delbos, *La philosophie française* (Paris, 1919).

Ad. Franck, *La Philosophie mystique en France* (Paris, 1866).

Leo Gershoy, *The French Revolution and Napoleon* (New York, 1939).

Daniel Mornet, *Les Origines intellectuelles de la Révolution française* (Paris, 1933).

Auguste Viatte, *Les Sources occultes du Romantisme* (Paris, 1928).

NOTES ON BONALD

1 Louis de Bonald, *Mélanges littéraires, politiques et philosophiques,* (Paris, 1852), pp. 31-32.

2 Louis de Bonald, *Oeuvres complètes,* I, (Paris, 1864) pp. 434-435.

3 Themes of Bonald's *Théorie du Pouvoir* and *Principe constitutif de la société.*
"Against that negative doctrine which supposes the absence of God in what

is nevertheless the work of God, Bonald proposes that of the real presence of God everywhere in the universe. It is true theism, complete theism, brought to bear against atheism." Charles Adam, *La philosophie en France* (Paris, 1894), p. 44.

[4] At the turn of the century, both the anti-philosophic *Annales Littéraires et Morales* and the gallican *Journal des Curés* refer frequently to Pascal as being superior to his eighteenth-century adversaries, and take pains to point out the distortions of Condorcet's *Eloge de Pascal*. Yet even for the *Annales Littéraires* it is Euler who serves as authority for the historical proofs of Christianity. During his affiliation with the *Mercure* and *Journal des Débats*, and in his *Mélanges littéraires, politiques et philosophiques*, Bonald is content to limit the public expression of his esteem for Pascal to the inclusion of his name among the authoritative opponents of the Enlightenment: "There have been no philosophic writings published in the last sixty years in which the authority of Montaigne, Pascal, La Bruyère, Montesquieu and Rousseau has not been recognized. Nowhere is the authority of Voltaire recognized, for he is without authority both as a philosopher and as a moralist." *Mélanges*, p 12.

[5] First numbers refer to the translation of the *Pensées* by H. F. Stewart, N. Y., 1950. The second number refers to the edition of The *Pensées* by Léon Brunschvicg, Paris. The quotation of Mme Périer is from Jacques Chevalier, *Pascal* (Paris, 1922), p. 158. See Jacques Maritain, *Ransoming The Time* (New York, 1941), pp. 33-52.

[6] Bonald, *Mélanges*, p. 338.

[7] Bonald, *Oeuvres* I, p. 550.

[8] *Ibid*, p. 320.

[9] *Ibid*, p. 392.

[10] Bonald, *Oeuvres* II, p. 230.

[11] Bonald, *Mélanges*, p. 245.

[12] Bonald, *Oeuvres* I, p. 130.

[13] *Ibid.*, p. 321.

NOTES ON MAISTRE

[1] For the relationship of Maistre to the founders of the *Conservateur*, consult F. Duine, *La Mennais, sa vie, ses idées, ses ouvrages* (Paris, 1922), Ch. IX.

[2] Joseph de Maistre, *Considérations sur la France*, Oeuvres I, (Lyon, 1891), Ch. 11.

[3] Maistre, *Considérations*, Oeuvres I, pp. 39-40.

[4] Maistre, *Sur la Souveraineté*, Oeuvres I, p. 375.

[5] G. Cagordan, *Joseph de Maistre* (Paris, 1894), p. 200.

[6] Maistre, *Principe générateur de la société, Oeuvres* I, p. 285.

[7] Buche explains Maistre's attitude towards the sciences in the light of his illuministic tendencies: "Against the materialism of the eighteenth century, the denial of the divine, science without a soul, the Voltairian scorn of miracles, he evokes with some malice and irony not the theology of the Middle Ages, but that thirst for mystery which has carried away some of his elegant contemporaries of good birth, like the marquis Claude de Saint-Martin and his disciples." *Ecole mystique de Lyon*, p. 14. If this were not belied by Maistre's praise of Saint Thomas at the end of the second *entretien* and by frequent references to Origen, we would at least feel the need for pointing out the clear subordination of the illumnism to Catholic doctrine in the eleventh *entretien*.

Bréhier, in his *Histore de la philosophie* II, 3, pp. 581-584, points out the philosophic origin of Maistre's attitude: "Against the empiricism (of Bacon, Locke, Voltaire and Diderot), he refers, as does Bonald, to the innate truths of Descartes: but we should examine in some detail the manner in which he understands it and re-introduces it." According to Bréhier, this is accomplished by a paradoxical juxtaposition of "the fixity of the species and the inexplicable nature of final causes." In the course of our study we shall see that Maistre's treatment of the second of these themes stems from a Pascalian sense of supra-rational causality. Faguet sees in Maistre only a passionate enemy of the rational: "The world is not rational, it is a system of profound, solid and vigorous absurdities. If Joseph de Maistre is so paradoxical, it is due to the fact that he sees the whole universe as a paradox." *Pol. et Mor.*, p. 42. Thus, empirically acquired data is of necessity false: A reason has a criterion which is evidence. If you wish to be almost sure of being mistaken and of receiving cruel deceptions from experience, you must consult this evidence." *Ibid.*, p. 40. With an important modification of this accusation, Dermenghem has come nearer the truth as we are to interpret it in this study: "The intellect cannot be satisfied by a narrow scientism which has just been denounced as a sterile confusion, which can give neither faith to the soul, nor an answer to the important questions raised by the mind, nor account for all phenomena, nor even bring about harmony within the city." E. Dermenghem, *Joseph de Maistre, mystique* (Paris, 1923), p. 126.

[8] Maistre, *Soirées de Saint-Pétersbourg, Oeuvres*, IV, p. 268.

[9] *Ibid.*, p. 257.

[10] Maistre, *Oeuvres* V, p. 76.

[11] The functions of the heart as instinct, source of knowledge and link with God, as indicated in the *Pensées*, is discussed by Ed. Benzécri, *l'Esprit humain selon Pascal* (Paris, 1939), p. 67.

[12] Maistre, *Soireés, Oeuvres* V, p. 128.

[13] *Ibid.*, p. 152.

[14] J. Reynaud, *Terre et Ciel* (Paris, 1864), 4th ed.

[15] Maistre, *Soirées, Oeuvres* V, p. 39.

[16] *Ibid.* V, p. 211.

[17] For Pascal's interpretation of the nature of the prophecies, see Jean Mesnard, *Pascal*, p. 164.

[18] Daniel-Rops, *Pascal et notre coeur* (Paris, 1948), p. 20.

[19] Faguet, *op.cit.*, p. 23.

[20] The phases of pessimism in the works of Vigny are taken from E. Dubedout, *Le sentiment chrétien dans la poésie romantique* (Paris, 1901), p. 178. For the relationship of this pessimism to Pascal and the Port-Royalists, see M. Citoleux, *Alfred de Vigny* (Paris, 1924), p. 240.

[21] This is the thesis of G. Goyau, *La pensée religieuse de Joseph de Maistre* (Paris, 1921), pp. 55-56. The same suggestion is made by Francoise Vermale, *Notes sur Joseph de Maistre inconnu* (Paris, 1921), pp. 95-96. We are attempting to show that the particular emphasis given to the role of will places Maistre in a more orthodox current of Christian thought as it derives from Pascal.

[22] Maistre, *Soirées, Oeuvres* IV, p. 212. Maistre's discovery of an ethical principle in the forms of human suffering is pointed out by Dermenghem, *Joseph de Maistre*, p. 216. The same theme is attributed to Maine de Brian and Bergson by Emile Lasbax, *Le Probléme du mal* (Paris, 1919), pp. 390-392. In our chapter on Biran we shall be able to examine the Pascalian resolution of suffering as it reappears in the nineteenth century.

NOTES ON LAMENNAIS

[1] B. Amoudru, *Des "Pascalins" aux "Pascalisants"* (Paris, 1936), p. 86.

[2] F. de Lamennais, *Essai sur l'Indifférence* (Paris nouvelle edition), I, p. 263.

[3] *Ibid.*, Vol. II, Chapters 1 and 2.

[4] *Ibid.*, Vol. II p. 105.

[5] *Chronique religieuse*, tome V, juillet, 1820, p. 270.

[6] *Mémorial catholique*, tome VI, juillet, 1826, p. 12. For a detailed study of this quarrel, see F.J.J. Vrijmoed, *Lamennais avant sa défection* (Paris, 1945).

[7] *Avenir,* 18 oct., 1830.

[8] *Ibid.,* 28 juin, 1831.

[9] F. de Lamennais, *Oeuvres complètes* (Paris, 1836-1837), tome XI, pp. 20-21.

[10] F. de Lamennais, *Esquisse d'une philosophie* (Paris, 1840), II, pp. 10-11.

[11] Alexandre Vinet, *Etudes sur Blaise Pascal* (Lausanne and Geneva, 1936), p. 194.

[12] Victor Giraud, *Pascal* (Fribourg, 1898), p. 72.

[13] George Boas, *French Philosophies of the Romantic Period* (Baltimore, 1925), p. 308.

[14] Pope Leo XIII, "Rerum Novarum," *The Papal Encyclicals* (N. Y., 1956), p. 167.

NOTES ON EARLY ROMANTIC WRITERS

[1] *Biographia Gallicas: The Lives of the most eminent French Writers of Both Sexes* (London, 1752), p. 124.

[2] Mme de Charrière recommends: "Read and re-read Pascal" and Mme de Beaumont confesses to Joubert with the spontaneous exaggeration of her day: "Do you know that if Port-Royal still existed, I should be in danger of fleeing to it?" The re-evaluation of Pascal by the émigrés in terms of their anguishing experiences is described by Jean-Jacques Demorest, "Pascal et les premiers Romantiques," *French Review,* Vol. XXII, May 1949, pp. 436-442. See also Betty Jane Eilersten, *Blaise Pascal in the Period 1789-1815,* Ph. D. Thesis, Universtiy of Illinois (Urbana, 1944).

[3] Charles-Julien de Chênedollé, *Extraits du Journal de Chênedollé* (1802-1833), par Mme de Samie (Caen, 1922), p. 160.

[4] C.-J. de Chênedollé, *Le Génie de l'homme* (Paris, 1807). The translations are my own, unless otherwise indicated.

[5] E. Dubedout, *Le Sentiment chrétien dans la poesie romantique* (Paris, 1901), p. 24.

[6] Charles G. Hill, "Vigny and Pascal," *PMLA,* December 1958, pp. 533-537.

[7] Albert Joseph George, *Pierre-Simon Ballanche, Precursor of Romanticism* (Syracuse, N. Y., 1945), p. 180.

[8] G. Frainnet, *Essai sur la philosophie de Pierre-Simon Ballanche* (Paris, 1903), p. 27.

[9] Jacques Roos, *Aspects Littéraires du Mysticisme Philosophique et l'influence de Boehme et de Swedenborg au début du Romantisme; William Blake, Novalis, Ballanche* (Strasbourg, 1951), pp. 392-393.

126

[10] Frainnet, op. cit., Chapter II.

[11] Buche, *Ecole mystique de Lyon*, p. 218.

[12] Ramon Guthrie and George E. Diller, *French Literature and Thought since the Revolution* (N.Y. 1942), p. 38.

[13] Paula Hey, *Chateaubriand und Pascal* (Bonn, 1937), p. 24.

[14] This interpretation has survived surprisingly intact for 150 years. Albert Guerard, in the Saturday Review of Literature, June 27, 1959, says of Pascal: "He failed. In despair he had recourse either to a wild gamble (his "wager"), immoral as all gambles are; or to the determined drugging of thought: 'Tell your beads, practice, it will stupify you.' His attempt is one of the noblest tragedies in human thought; his glorious failure is a lesson which no honest thinker can ignore." p. 18. The "glorious failure" image does not seem quite as appropriate in the twentieth century as at the beginning of the nineteenth.

[15] Pascal said in the same vein: " . . . what is nature for animals we call misery for man; by which we recognize that his nature being today similar to that of animals, he has fallen from a better nature which was proper for him formerly" (Br. p. 512). Pascal's image of man as a "depossessed king" is reflected in Chateaubriand's "crumbled palace."

[16] In his own day, the *Annales littéraires et morales* linked Chateaubriand with Pascal in the critique of the new ethical empiricism: "It is a very strange mania of those self-styled thinkers, of those single-minded fanatics who want to measure everything by compass, who see no beauty except that of numbers and who would make religion a mere algebraic equation. This is not the way that the great geometrist Pascal thought when he said that if the mind has its order of proceding by principles and demonstrations, the heart also has its own. Now, it is these principles and demonstrations of the heart that M. de Chateaubriand proposed to establish by showing us that religion alone is the source of the greatest thoughts and feelings and that the farther we depart from it, the farther we go from nature, virtue, good taste and true beauty, and these principles and demonstrations are worth more than those cold analyses, those fine-spun calculations, those chemical transformations and other such ingredients as our empirical sophists have wanted to work into the reconstruction of our happiness and our ethics" III, p. 397.

This analysis is extended by Victor Giraud, *Le Christianisme de Chateaubriand* (Paris, 1925), II, p. 14.

Also pertinent to this study are the following:

Ch. de Chênedollé, *Oeuvres complètes* (Paris, 1864), Nouvelle édition précédée d'une notice par Sainte-Beuve.

Pierre-Simon Ballanche, *Oeuvres* (Paris and Geneva, 1830), 4 vols.

Oeuvres complètes de M. le Vicomte de Chateaubriand (Paris, 1836).

F.-R. de Chateaubriand, *Vie de Rancé* (Paris, 1920).

J. Evans, *The Unselfish Egoist: a life of Joseph Joubert* (London, N. Y., 1947).

Auguste Viatte, *Claude-Julien Bredin* (Paris, 1927). Correspondance philosophique et littéraire avec Ballanche.

Alfred Marquiset, *Ballanche et Mme d'Hautefeuille, lettres inédites* (Paris, 1912).

Madeleine Dempsey, *A contribution to the study of the sources of the Genie du Christianisme* (Paris, 1928).

A. Dollinger, *Les Etudes historiques de Chateaubriand* (Paris, 1932).

Marie-Jeanne Durry, *La Vieillesse de Chateaubriand*, 1830-1848. (Paris, 1933).

H. Gillot, *Chateaubriand* (Paris, 1934).

Victor Giraud, *De Chateaubriand à Brunetière,* essai sur le mouvement catholique en Frances au XIXe siècle (Paris, 1938).

Carlos Lynes, "Chateaubriand as a critic of French Literature," *Johns Hopkins Studies in Romance Literatures and Languages,* Vol. XLVI (Baltimore, 1946).

Paul Pierrot, "Chateaubriand et Pascal -1'influence des *Pensées* sur le *Génie du Christianisme,*" *Revue Générale* (Brussels, 1829).

See also:

Henri Peyre, "Friends and Foes of Pascal in France Today," *Yale French Studies* XII (Fall-Winter 1953).

P. André, "Pascal devant la critique moderne," *Le Monde Francais* (Dec. 1950), pp. 431-455.

FOOTNOTES ON ACADEMICIANS AND MORALISTS

[1] The discussion of Rivarol has appeared in *CRITICISM*, Vol. I, No. 3, Summer, 1959, under the title: "Rivarol's *Morale Indépendante* and Pascal."

[2] Biographical material from Roger Langeron's *Un conseiller secret de Louis XVIII, Royer-Collard* (Paris, 1956), p. 8.

[3] Quotation from Charles Jourdain in *Journal de l'instruction publique,* 27 nov., 1858. Prosper Alfaric, *Laromiguère et son école* (Paris, 1929), p. 232.

[4] George Boas, *French Philosophies of the Romantic Period,* Baltimore, 1925

In his *Politiques et Moralistes du 19ᵉ siècle* (Paris, 1891), Emile Faguet
points out that "Royer-Collard had the deepest admiration for the
Pensées of Pascal; apparently he did not neglect the *Provinciales*." Vol. I,
p. 303.

5 Joseph-Marie de Gérando, *Histoire Comparée des systèmes de philosophie*
(Paris, 1804), 3 vols., Introduction, p. XXVII. We shall refer to the
Paris edition of 1847, Vols. V-VIII.

6 Jean-Philibert Damiron, *Essai sur l'Histoire de la philosophie en France, au
XIXᵉ siècle* (Paris, 1854), II, p. 403.

7 Basil Willey, *The Eighteenth Century Background* (London, 1946), p. 62.

8 Charles Frankel, *The Faith of Reason* (New York, 1948), p. 69.

9 Immanuel Kant, *Fundamental Principles of the Metaphysic of Morals*
Chicago, 1949), pp. 74-75.

10 These comparisons have been variously suggested by A. de la Valette-
Monbrun, *Maine de Biran, critique et disciple de Pascal* (Paris, 1914), p.
137, and in his introduction to Biran's *Journal Intime*, p. XLIV, by Victor
Delbos, *Figures et Doctrines* (Paris, 1918), p. 310, and by Pierre Tisserand,
Ouvres de Maine de Biran (Paris, 1920), Vol. I, p. XVII. *Maine de Biran,
Sa Vie et ses Pensées*, Naville, p. 123. Ernest Naville, (ed.), *Maine de
Biran* (Paris, 1857), p. 123.

12 *Oeuvres*, Vol. XIV, p. 79, note *Sur l'idée d'existence*.

13 Naville, *op. cit.*, p. 128.

14 *Oeuvres*, Vol. I, p. 31.

15 Naville, *op. cit.*, pp. 126-127.

16 *Oeuvres*, Vol. I, p. 97.

17 *Ibid.*, p. 60.

18 *Ibid.*, p. 220.

19 *Ibid.*, Vol. II, p. 26.

20 *Ibid.*, Vol. II, pp. 75-76. See also p. 90.

21 *Ibid.*, pp. 196-198.

22 Victor Delbos, *Maine de Biran et son Oeuvre philosophique* (Paris, 1931),
p. 286.

23 *Oeuvres*, Vol. III, p. 238.

24 *Ibid.*, Vol. XIV, p. 318.

25 Philip P. Hallie, *Maine de Biran, Reformer of Empiricism, 1766-1824*
Cambridge, 1959), pp. 112 and 125.

26 John Locke, *An Essay Concerning Human Understanding, The English
Philosophers*, p. 310.

[27] *The English Philosophers*, Jeremy Bentham, *Introduction to the Principles of Morals and Legislation*, p. 785.

[28] Denis Diderot, *Oeuvres choisies*, 2 Vols, (Paris, Garnier), Vol II, p. 92.

[29] Voltaire, *Dictionnaire philosophique* in 2 Vols., ed. by Julien Benda (Paris), p. 91.

[30] Frederick Copleston, S. J., *Arthur Schopenhauer, Philosopher of Pessimism* (Burns, Oates and Washbourne Ltd., 1947), p. 152.

[31] The naturalist position is stated by Vergilius Ferm, "Varieties of Naturalism," *A History of Philosophical System* (New York, 1950), p. 438.

[32] *Oeuvres*, Vol. X, pp. 65-66.

[33] *Ibid.*, p. 374.

[34] Karl Jaspers, *Reason and Anti-Reason in our Time* (New Haven, 1952), pp. 53-54.

[35] *Oeuvres*, Vol. X, p. 277.

[36] *Ibid.*, Vol. XII, p. 12.

[37] *Ibid.*, Vol. X, p. 354.

[38] *Ibid.*, Vol. IX, p. 605.

[39] The quotations are taken from *Oeuvres*, Vol. XI, pp. 391-401, Vol. XIV, p. 338, and Vol. X, pp. 65-66.

[40] Naville, *op. cit.*, p. 209.

[41] *Oeuvres*, Vol. XIV, p. 376.

[42] The quotations in this paragraph are taken from *Oeuvres*, Vol. XIV, pp. 374-395.

[43] *Oeuvres*, Vol. XI, p. LVII. Valette-Monbrun, *op. cit.*, p. 283.

[44] Naville, *op. cit.*, p. 238.

[45] George Le Roy, *L'expérience de l'effort et de la grâce chez Maine de Biran* (Paris, 1937), p. 379.

[46] *Oeuvres*, Vol. XII, p |289.

[47] The quotations in this paragraph are from *Maine de Biran*, Naville, pp. 247-253.

[48] Pascal's *Pensées* are taken from the Brunschvicg edition, p. 302 and p. 562. The translations are my own.

[49] *Oeuvres*, Vol. XII, p. 298.

[50] *Ibid.*, Vol. XIV, p. 397.

[51] Naville, *op. cit.*, pp. 266-268.

[52] *Oeuvres*, Vol. XIV, p. 382.

[53] The quotations in this paragraph are from *Oeuvres*, Vol. XIV, pp. 385-399.

[54] A. de la Valette-Monbrun, *op. cit.*, p. 283.

Victor Delbos, *Figures et Doctrines*, pp. 325-326.

B. Amoudru, *La Vie Posthume des "Pensées"* (Paris, 1936), p. 95.

G. Leroy, *op. cit.*, pp. 427-428.

[55] These quotations are from the Brunschvicg edition of the *Pensées*, p. 369 and p. 449.

[56] Most of the editions of the *Pensées* available to the Romantic philosophers were constructed along the lines of the Port-Royal or Bossut editions. The Renouard editions appeared in 1803 and 1812. Those of P. Didot l'aîné appeared in 1817 and 1818. The Frantin edition (Dijon, Lagier, 1835; Paris, 1853 and 1870) was the first attempting to reconstruct the plan of the *Pensées*. Victor Cousin's discovery of the autograph copy of the *Pensées* (1842) lead to the printing of the Faugère edition of 1844 and eventually to the famous Havet edition in 1852.

Index